EatingWell
quick + clean

Grilled Salmon with
Tomatoes & Basil *(page 158)*

EatingWell®

quick + clean

100 easy recipes for better meals every day

THE EDITORS OF EATINGWELL

Houghton Mifflin Harcourt

BOSTON NEW YORK 2017

For information about permission to reproduce selections
from this book, write to trade.permissions@hmhco.com or to
Permissions, Houghton Mifflin Harcourt Publishing Company,
3 Park Avenue, 19th Floor, New York, New York 10016.
www.hmhco.com

Library of Congress Cataloging-in-Publication Data is available.

ISBN 978-0-544-92550-2 (pbk.)

ISBN 978-0-544-91933-4 (ebk.)

Book design by Jan Derevjanik

Printed in China

SCP 10 9 8 7 6 5 4 3 2 1

On the cover: Sugar Snap Pea Salad, page 169

EatingWell®

Editor-in-Chief: Jessie Price

Creative Director: James Van Fleteren

Food Editor: Jim Romanoff

Managing Editor: Wendy S. Ruopp

Nutrition Editor: Brierley Wright, M.S., R.D.

Senior Food Editor: Carolyn Malcoun

Test Kitchen Manager: Stacy Fraser

Associate Food Editor: Breana Lai, M.P.H., R.D.

Recipe Developer & Tester: Carolyn Casner

Nutrition Consultant: Jill Cerreta, M.S., R.D.

Art Director: Maria Emmighausen

Research Editor: Anne Treadwell

Associate Nutrition Editor: Julia Westbrook

Editorial Assistant: Lucy M. Casale

EatingWell Quick & Clean

Project Manager: Leslie Jonath, Connected Dots Media

Project Editor: Kim Laidlaw

Contributing Writers: Shaun Dreisbach; Stephanie Clarke, M.S., R.D. & Willow Jarosh, M.S., R.D., C&J Nutrition; Anne Treadwell

Contributing Copy Editors and Proofreaders: Ivy McFadden and Anne Treadwell

Principal Photographer: Erin Kunkel

Stylists: Lillian Kang (food), Natasha Kolenko (props)

Contributing Photographers: Erica Allen, Peter Ardito, Marty Baldwin, Leigh Beisch, Ken Burris, Karla Conrad, Penny De Los Santos, Carin Krasner, Bryan McCay, Blaine Moats, Leah Nash, Helen Norman, Andrew Scrivani, Ellen Silverman, Joe Vaughn, Jeb Wallace-Brodeur

Cover Photography: Helen Norman; *styling:* Frances Boswell (food), Ayesha Patel (props)

Illustrations: Emma Dibben

Designer: Jan Derevjanik

Indexer: Elizabeth Parson

Houghton Mifflin Harcourt

Editorial Director: Cindy Kitchel

Executive Editor: Anne Ficklen

Editorial Associate: Molly Aronica

Managing Editor: Marina Padakis Lowry

Art Director: Tai Blanche

Production Director: Tom Hyland

contents

Skillet Swiss Steak (*page 120*)

clean,
the *eatingwell* way

There are few greater pleasures in life than fresh, delicious food: a handful of berries straight off the bush, still warm from the sun, or a bowl of made-from-scratch pasta with just-harvested veggies. That is what eating clean is all about. And even though "clean" has become a big buzzword lately, it is not a passing trend—it's a *movement*. The mission? To get back to basics and eat whole, nourishing foods that are as close as possible to the way nature made them—you know, the way we used to eat before the invention of sliced white bread, flavored yogurt and cheap, easy takeout. Above all, clean eating is not a diet; it is a lifestyle—a way of considering what you put on your plate so you can feel and look better not just for now, but *forever*.

Maybe clean-eating is fairly new to you, or maybe or it's just part of who you are. At *EatingWell*, it has always been a core objective of ours: we celebrate fresh food that is both nutritious and incredibly delicious. So we designed this book to be your go-to resource on all things clean. We've included guidelines on what foods to enjoy and which to steer clear of. And, of course, there are recipes—more than 100 of them that have been tested in our Test Kitchen and vetted by our team of registered dietitians. The best part is that they're all easy and speedy to make. Our goal is to show you that eating clean doesn't have to be complicated or take a lot of extra time. You can do it even with a busy schedule!

But let's back up for a moment and talk about what *exactly* it means to eat clean. The basic concept is to eat a primarily plant-based diet filled with fruits, vegetables, whole grains, dairy and small amounts of meat and fish that are minimally processed and as free from potentially harmful substances—including pesticides, additives, preservatives, unhealthy fats and large amounts of sugar and salt—as possible. It also means avoiding highly refined foods with ingredients you'd need a lab technician to help you pronounce.

Within that broad definition, however, there are

many shades of gray. Surf around online and you'll find that everyone—from doctors and nutritionists to bloggers and big-name health sites—has a different take on the basic tenets of clean eating. Some go hard-core clean—whizzing up green juice every morning, eating organic everything and making foods like hummus, pasta sauce and nut butter from scratch instead of buying them at the market. (A noble idea, but exhausting-sounding!) Others insist on cutting entire food groups, like dairy, or going vegan.

We take a sensible, science-backed approach in our guidelines, which we'll spell out for you in this chapter—one that focuses on whole foods in a way that's doable no matter what your lifestyle or budget, and offers room for you to choose a definition of clean eating that best fits your needs. Because the truth is, even if you only take a few steps toward eating cleaner—cutting back on processed foods, for example, or eating more fruits and veggies (and, if it works for you, buying a few organic)—it can still positively impact your health.

So what are the benefits of eating clean—or even just cleaner? For starters, it can help you live a long and healthy life. Research shows that this way of eating helps reduce inflammation in the body and, in turn,

lowers your risk for every major disease—from cancer and cardiovascular disease to diabetes and dementia. Many devotees also find that it makes them feel better in general—more clearheaded, energetic, even less stressed. And there's good evidence that eating clean can help you easily maintain an ideal weight—or drop some pounds, if you need to. For example, a study of overweight people found that those who made an effort to clean up their diets as advised by their doctor—by eating very little processed stuff and lots of nutrient-dense fruits, veggies, nuts and whole grains—lost an average of 31 pounds over the course of a year.

The best part about eating clean is that it has nothing to do with sacrifice. It's about *reward*: rewarding your body with wonderful food that will make you feel better and live a healthier life, and rewarding your taste buds with fresh flavors that are guaranteed to bring you far more pleasure than any fast-food burger or 100-calorie pack of cookies ever could. What's not to love about a plan like that? But before you dash into the kitchen and start whipping up our delicious quick and clean recipes (they start on page 22), read on for all the details about how to eat in a more as-nature-intended way.

the 7 principles of clean

1 LOAD UP ON PRODUCE

When it comes to fruits and vegetables, you probably know the general drill: fill at least half your plate with produce each time you sit down to a meal, make more meals totally meatless and aim to get in a broad variety of fruits and veggies (the whole "eat the rainbow" thing). Yet according to the Centers for Disease Control and Prevention, 76 percent of Americans don't get enough fruit each day and a whopping 87 percent aren't eating enough servings of veg. So if you're falling short—and clearly you've got lots of company—it's time to redouble your efforts to eat more produce.

Clean produce, that is. Get this: Conventional farmers in the U.S. have more than 1,400 chemicals—pesticides, herbicides, fertilizers and fungicides—they can use on their crops to promote growth and protect their plants from critters and disease. And consuming these toxins has been linked to a host of different health problems, including breast, colon, lung and stomach cancers, asthma, birth defects and Hodgkin's and non-Hodgkin's lymphoma. (To be clear: We're talking about synthetic chemicals here. There are natural pest repellents that organic farmers are allowed to use—and much lower levels of them end up on your produce.) But before you freak out and think you have to buy all organic, all the time, know this: if you only have the ability to buy some things organic, the ones to home in on are the so-called Dirty Dozen™ that have been found to be the most contaminated when grown conventionally, according to the Environmental Working Group, a nonprofit organization. EWG estimates that just by eating organic versions of the Dirty Dozen, you can reduce your pesticide exposure by 80 percent. Pretty significant! Of course, if you want to get all your fruit and veg this way, please—go for it. But it's not necessary. In fact, EWG has pinpointed some types of produce that are typically so low in pesticides they may not be worth the extra expense of going organic. They're called the Clean Fifteen™. (Go to *ewg.org* for the most up-to-date information.)

There are also other benefits you can reap by loading up on produce: high fruit and vegetable consumption has been shown to significantly reduce your risk for a number of chronic diseases, including high blood pressure, type 2 diabetes, heart disease, obesity and cancer. The fiber in whole produce also helps keep your microbiome (the collection of good bacteria that live in your gastrointestinal tract) humming happily along, which can reduce your risk for autoimmune diseases, fight off pathogens and infections and even improve your mood. And the benefits kick in *like that* when you start eating a more plant-forward diet. A Harvard study that put people on either an entirely animal-based diet or on one that was exclusively plant-based, then compared their gut bacteria, found that just one day was enough to dramatically shift their microbiome, with the animal-diet group showing growth of microorganisms linked to inflammatory bowel disease.

Do You Need to Do a Detox Diet?

Detox diets—whether it's a juice cleanse, supplements or sticking to a super-limited number of foods—are really just a trendy new way of saying "crash diet." Any weight you lose is mainly water—which means you'll gain it all back the moment you go back to your normal eating habits. And it actually doesn't remove any additional toxins that your body wouldn't naturally eliminate on its own—through your liver, kidneys and lungs. But you can help *support* your body's detox process by eating nutrient-rich foods that are high in soluble fiber—such as apples, oatmeal and eggplant—because the fiber binds to toxins and helps ferry them out of your body. Plus, fiber in general picks up potentially harmful chemicals, like BPA, mercury and pesticides, and moves them quickly through your system. The faster they go through you, the less chance they have to hang out and cause harm. Eating a high-fiber diet will also keep you regular—and give you that feeling of lightness that people like about detox diets. There's also evidence that certain compounds in broccoli and cilantro, as well as selenium-rich foods like garlic and mushrooms, can aid in the detox process.

2 GO WHOLE GRAIN

If you're wondering what qualifies as a "clean" whole grain, here's a quick primer: The most *whole*, whole grains are those that have barely been touched since they were harvested—foods like wheat berries, quinoa, amaranth, oats and wild rice. A whole grain contains all three parts of the kernel: the bran (the fibrous outer shell), the germ (the nutrient-packed embryo) and the endosperm. The endosperm is the starchy part that contains the bulk of the carbohydrates and is usually all that remains when grains are refined. Refined grains have had their outer bran shell and germ removed; foods made from them include white pasta and white bread.

Some clean-eating proponents recommend only eating the wholest whole grains, as opposed to items simply made from whole grain (like whole-wheat bread and whole-wheat pasta). If that's the route you want to take, go for it. Personally, we couldn't live without a hearty sandwich on great whole-wheat bread now and then. Finding clean versions of items like bread, cereal, crackers and pasta can be tricky, though, because every label seems to scream "whole-grain!" these days—and they're definitely not all created equal. (For the record, all the recipes in this book use 100 percent whole grains, so there's no decoding necessary!) Here are our criteria for selecting high-quality, clean whole grains when you shop and cook on your own.

What to Look For

- For items like pasta, bread and crackers, the first ingredient listed should be whole grains or whole wheat.

- The ingredients list should be short, and only contain things that you can identify as actual food.

What to Avoid

- Don't fall for words like multigrain, stone-ground or 100% wheat on the front of the package—they're not always whole-grain. Scope out the ingredients to know for sure. And just because it's brown doesn't guarantee it's healthy, either. Often, manufacturers add molasses (ahem, *sugar*) or caramel color to make it look better than it actually is.

- If it's got a lot of added sugars or you find sugar listed toward the top of the ingredient list *(see Sugar's Many Aliases, page 17)*, leave it on the shelf. The same rules apply for sodium.

Swapping some of the refined carbs in your diet for whole grains can do your health a world of good. Research has found that the fiber, antioxidants and whole-grain-only phytonutrients that fight inflammation can reduce your risk for a host of diseases, including heart disease, diabetes and cancer. There's also good evidence linking whole-grain consumption to weight loss—and the ability to maintain a healthy weight for the long haul. The fiber in whole grains can even help clear out any toxins that do make it into your system *(see Do You Need to Do a Detox Diet, page 10)*. Because no matter how clean you try to eat, there's no way to totally avoid them.

Refined grains, on the other hand, have the opposite effect on your health. Aside from having the nutrition stripped out of them, processed carbs—such as white bread and anything made with refined flour—have been shown to mess up the balance of gut bacteria (your microbiome) and promote disease-inducing inflammation. And research shows that a surprising number of calories in our diets—40 percent!—come from refined carbs. So even cutting just some of the junk will serve you well.

MYTH OR TRUTH?
Going gluten-free is cleaner.

Myth. It isn't necessary to cut out gluten (the protein found in wheat, rye and barley) if you're not sensitive to it. There is a faction of clean-eating proponents who consider gluten a toxin—in part because wheat has been bred to contain way more gluten than it used to, which they claim causes inflammation. But there's no hard evidence to support this idea that gluten is harmful to us. Some research even counters the notion that wheat has more gluten these days. That said, there is evidence that the reactions people think are caused by gluten—brain fog, digestive issues like gas, bloating and constipation—may actually be triggered by a sensitivity to nongluten wheat proteins or even the carbohydrates in the wheat. So, in that case, cutting out wheat (but not just because of the gluten) may help ease symptoms. But those same hard-to-digest carbohydrates (collectively called FODMAPs—fermentable oligo-di-monosaccharides and polyols) are also found in a host of other foods, from onions to beans to apples.

3 EAT LESS MEAT

More and more science suggests that cutting back on meat is healthier for both your body and the environment (more on that last part on page 20). In fact, the evidence is so compelling that *EatingWell* has an entire cookbook on going meatless, called *Fast & Flavorful Meatless Meals*.

We're not suggesting you swear off cheeseburgers or convert to veganism, but going meatless more often is known to keep blood pressure and cholesterol levels down and reduce your risk of heart disease, type 2 diabetes and certain cancers. Research also shows that cutting back on meat can help naturally keep your weight in check, while at the same time helping you get more fiber, healthy fats and vitamins and minerals—specifically C, E, folate, potassium and magnesium.

Don't worry about not getting enough protein in your diet, either. Despite the protein frenzy, the average American already gets way more protein than needed, anyway. The recommendation for healthy adults is about 0.8 gram of protein per kilogram of body weight—which translates to roughly 56 grams a day for men and 46 grams for women. But men eat nearly double that amount, while women get one-and-a-half times the recommendation. Plus, it's actually very easy to meet your daily quota through other sources, like beans and nuts (see the chart at right for some top protein-rich options).

Eggs are another great vegetarian source of protein. If you're interested in buying eggs from hens raised humanely and lacking synthetic inputs, see page 255 for our egg buyer's guide. Dairy is also a healthful vegetarian protein source. Don't shy away from full-fat versions—they often have a simpler ingredient list and the extra fat can help with satiety. In fact, some research has found that people who eat full-fat dairy tend to be leaner—while those who go for the fat-free versions typically have higher BMIs. Remember to scope out the ingredients lists on items like yogurt to make sure you're not getting unnecessary additives—like carrageenan—or boatloads of added sugar. Ounce for ounce, some flavored yogurts have more added sugar than soda!

When you do eat meat, choose beef, pork and poultry that hasn't been pumped full of antibiotics. The overuse of antibiotics in animal farming is leading to the rise of superbugs that can cause infections in humans that antibiotics are no longer effective at treating. With beef, look for meat from animals not treated with hormones (hormones aren't allowed in animals being raised for chicken and pork). Even better if the animal also ate the way it would in the wild, like beef that was grass-fed, which actually makes the meat

Top Protein Sources—That Aren't Meat

Yes, the list extends way beyond tofu (which clocks in at about 9 grams per 3-ounce serving, for the record). Take a look!

THE FOOD	AMOUNT OF PROTEIN
Greek yogurt	23 grams per cup
Lentils	4 grams per 1/4 cup (cooked)
Beans (chickpeas, black beans, etc.)	4 grams per 1/4 cup (cooked)
Cottage cheese	14 grams per 1/2 cup
Hemp seeds	4 grams per 1 tablespoon
Chia seeds	3 grams per 1 tablespoon
Edamame	5 grams per 1/4 cup (shelled)
Green peas	8 grams per cup
Quinoa	8 grams per cup (cooked)
Peanut butter	3.5 grams per 1 tablespoon
Almonds	3 grams per 1/2 ounce
Eggs	6 grams per large egg

more nutritious. Research shows that meat from grass-fed cattle, for example, contains 47 percent more healthy omega-3 fats than meat from their conventionally raised counterparts. *(See Buyer's Guide, page 248, for more information on meat and poultry labels.)*

As for fish, choose varieties that are low in mercury—which includes catfish, crab, clams, salmon, scallops, shrimp, tilapia, trout and skipjack tuna. (Go to *nrdc.org/mercury* for a full list of low- and high-mercury fish.)

Yes, many of these meat and seafood choices come with higher price tags, but if you're eating less anyway, it's not going to break the bank. Think of meat and seafood as a *small component of* your meal—rather than the main event—which also offsets the added expense. Keep portions to 3 ounces of cooked meat and 4 ounces of cooked fish.

Another key move: cut back as much as you can on processed meats, like cold cuts, bacon and sausage, because they contain preservatives like nitrates, which may raise your risk of cancer, according to a recent review of more than 800 studies by the World Health Organization.

MYTH OR TRUTH?

Dairy causes inflammation.

Myth. Some clean-eating plans recommend ditching dairy—citing that some research has linked it to inflammation in the body, even in people who aren't sensitive or intolerant to lactose.

However, a Canadian review of studies on the subject concluded that eating dairy does not promote inflammation—and, in fact, may actually help *reduce* it. Experts agree more research needs to be done, but in the meantime, as long as dairy doesn't bother you (i.e., cause gastrointestinal symptoms like gas and bloating) there's no reason to give it up.

4 WATCH OUT FOR PROCESSED FOODS

Technically, any food that passes through human hands (or mechanized ones) before it gets to you is "processed"—from organic eggs to neon-orange packaged snacks. But what we're talking about here are processed foods (like the aforementioned orange ones). There's nothing inherently wrong with processing—after all, every time we take raw food and chop, mix or cook it, we're processing it. It's just that much of the processed food at the supermarket these days is a quagmire of not-so-great added ingredients. Here are the hallmarks of the sorts of processed food you want to avoid:

- It's loaded with sugar and refined flour.

- It has a long ingredient list.

- It doesn't resemble its former self (think: chicken nuggets, as opposed to chicken breasts).

- It contains ingredients you don't recognize as an actual food—like aspartame, Blue 2 and whatever the heck TBHQ is.

- It has partially hydrogenated oils (translation: unhealthy man-made trans fats).

On the other hand, processed foods made with a few simple ingredients (pasta made from just flour and water, for example) are fine, as are certain crackers (grains, salt, oil) and cheese (milk, rennet, salt). Even potato chips made with canola oil and a little sea salt pass the clean test. As for things like salad dressing, pasta sauce, mayo, hummus and other convenience foods, if you can make your own—so it's fresh and you can control exactly what goes into it—that's great. But don't stress if you simply don't have the time or inclination. Just choose versions with the simplest ingredient list you can find. They're out there!

Getting mega-refined foods out of your life may be one of the most important clean-eating improvements you can make. Research shows that as they've become a bigger and bigger part of our lives—one recent study found they comprise more than half the calories in our diets!—rates of heart disease, diabetes and obesity have climbed correspondingly. It's not a coincidence.

What's more, there's evidence that processed foods promote weight gain on several levels. In a *Food & Nutrition Research* study, for example, participants ate a sandwich made either from multigrain bread and Cheddar cheese or from white bread and processed cheese. When the researchers measured how much energy participants expended digesting and absorbing the food, they discovered that the group that ate the multigrain sandwich burned nearly twice as many calories to break it down compared to the group that ate the highly processed sandwich. The reason? Our bodies handle processed and unprocessed foods differently. In the case of refined grains, for instance, a machine has already done the work of stripping away the tougher-to-digest parts of the wheat—the bran and germ—which leaves less work for your body to do. And over time, that can lead to weight gain.

Limiting packaged foods will also cut down on your exposure to phthalates—a group of chemicals used to make soft plastics. Research suggests that they act as endocrine disruptors, interfering with the body's hormone systems and possibly causing reproductive abnormalities, as well as problems with fertility, and increasing your risk for diabetes and cancer. Also, when you buy processed foods like ready-to-eat beans or vegetable broth, go for ones in "BPA-free" cans, cartons or jars. Bisphenol A is a chemical used in some plastics and in can linings to prevent corrosion and keep the contents from tasting tinny. It can leach into food, and studies show that consuming it can lead to early puberty, reproductive irregularities,

cardiovascular and neurological damage and obesity. Cleanup needed in Aisle 5!

Many food manufacturers have taken the BPA out of their products, but recent research suggests that the replacement chemicals—bisphenol S (BPS) and bisphenol F (BPF) are two common ones—may be just as harmful, if not worse, than BPA. The upside is that BPS may be less likely to leach into food when heated in the container. We do call for canned beans in our recipes because they're quick, convenient and the easiest option to find. But you can find ready-to-eat versions in boxes (called Tetra Paks), glass jars or cans that aren't lined with plastic containing this chemical—or buy dried beans if you have time to soak them overnight before cooking them to use in a recipe.

5 LIMIT SUGAR

Entire books have been written about the evils of too much added sugar, but here's the helicopter view on this sweet ingredient: Eating sugar—or refined carbs like white flour, which your body converts to sugar—causes your insulin levels to spike. When insulin levels roller-coaster over time, it could lead to insulin resistance, upping your risk for diabetes. Sugar also promotes inflammation, which may raise your risk for diabetes, and even cancer. And the stuff is absolutely *everywhere*—not just in sweet foods, like fro-yo. It's added to salad dressings, pasta sauces, soup, ketchup, breads, barbecue sauces, yogurts, even your morning mocha latte.

According to the American Heart Association, women should have no more than 100 calories of added sugar a day (that's about 6 teaspoons); for men the limit is 150 calories (about 9 teaspoons). What the average American actually gets: around three times that amount—22 teaspoons' worth a day. To be clear, we're talking about *added* sugars here. You don't need to worry so much about the sugars that occur naturally in foods like fruit and milk, because these foods often contain another substance—such as fiber or fat—that blunts the effect of sugar on insulin levels. Thanks to new labeling laws, you'll soon be able to tell how much of a food's sugars are added. Compare labels at the store and go for versions with the lowest amount of added sugars—particularly in savory foods that sugar has no business being in, anyway.

And don't be fooled into leaning on artificial sweeteners to fill the sugar void. Some evidence suggests they shift levels of gut bacteria in a way that promotes glucose intolerance, which can increase obesity and diabetes risk similarly to the way sugar can. So consume these no-calorie sweeteners sparingly too. They're showing up in a surprising number of products these days—from energy drinks to salad dressings—as food manufacturers sub them in to take down the amount of added sugars and make items appear better than they are. We'll say it yet again: Read those labels!

Rest assured that all the savory foods in this book are free of sugar—even the desserts are light on the stuff. We use it sparingly, when needed, to make baked goods tender or crispy around the edges—or to add a specific flavor, like the wonderful toasty taste that brown sugar lends to sweets.

Sugar's Many Aliases

There are actually at least *64 different names* for this sweet guy—and no matter what form it takes, it's treated pretty much the same way in your body. Here are some of the many ways you might see it on food labels (in addition to the actual word "sugar," of course):

1. Anhydrous dextrose
2. Agave
3. Agave nectar
4. Beet sugar
5. Brown sugar (light and dark brown)
6. Cane juice
7. Cane juice solids
8. Cane sugar
9. Cane syrup
10. Carob syrup
11. Caster sugar
12. Coconut sugar
13. Confectioners' sugar
14. Corn syrup
15. Corn syrup solids
16. Crystalline fructose
17. Date sugar
18. Demerara sugar
19. Dextran
20. Dextrose
21. Dehydrated cane juice
22. Evaporated cane juice
23. Evaporated cane syrup
24. Evaporated sugar cane
25. Fructose
26. Fructose crystals
27. Fruit juice concentrate
28. Fruit juice crystals
29. Glazing sugar
30. Glucose
31. Glucose syrup
32. Golden sugar
33. Golden syrup
34. Granulated sugar
35. High-fructose corn syrup (HFCS)
36. Honey
37. Icing sugar
38. Invert sugar
39. Invert syrup
40. King's syrup
41. Lactose
42. Maple sugar
43. Maple syrup
44. Maltose
45. Malt sugar
46. Malt syrup
47. Molasses
48. Muscovado sugar
49. Nectar
50. Pancake syrup
51. Panocha
52. Powdered sugar
53. Raw sugar
54. Refiners' syrup
55. Sorghum syrup
56. Sucanat
57. Sucrose
58. Sugar
59. Superfine sugar
60. Table sugar
61. Treacle
62. Turbinado sugar
63. White sugar
64. Yellow sugar

MYTH OR TRUTH?
Natural sweeteners are better for you.

Myth. Natural sweeteners like maple syrup and raw honey are often recommended in clean-eating diets, but whether made by bees or refined by humans—like table sugar and high-fructose corn syrup—they all behave the same way in your body. In other words, sugar is sugar is sugar. That said, natural sweeteners like honey and maple syrup deliver small amounts of beneficial minerals and antioxidants.

6 KEEP AN EYE ON SODIUM

Salt has the magical ability to make almost any food—even sweet ones—taste better. (Salted caramel gelato, anyone?) And you need a certain amount of salt in your diet to maintain the fluid balance in your body and help it work the way it should. But in too high a dose, of course, salt can wreak some serious havoc, including raising blood pressure in people who are sensitive and increasing your risk of heart attack and stroke. And the average American is getting way more than they should—a staggering 3,400 milligrams a day. The Dietary Guidelines recommends keeping sodium intake below 2,300 milligrams daily, which is equivalent to about a teaspoon of salt. And the American Heart Association says an ideal limit would be even lower: 1,500 milligrams.

It might surprise you that our sodium problem isn't because of overenthusiastic saltshaker use. The vast majority of our intake—almost 80 percent—comes from all the convenience foods we eat that have been loaded with salt, either to improve the flavor or act as a preservative. You'll naturally curb your intake just by virtue of cutting back on processed foods, but it's also a good idea to read labels to make sure you're not getting more sodium than you bargained for, because it's hidden in some unexpected places, from breakfast cereal to canned beans. As with sugar, sodium can show up on the ingredients list under many different guises, including monosodium glutamate (MSG), sodium chloride, sodium nitrite and made-in-a-lab-sounding words, such as disodium EDTA.

In addition to scoping out the ingredients list, look at the Nutrition Facts Panel. Compare products and choose ones with the least amount of sodium. Some foods, like broth and soy sauce, are unavoidably salty, and that's OK. Again, they're not the biggest culprits when it comes to sodium intake.

To keep sodium under control in our recipes, we use plenty of spices, herbs and citrus to make things taste good. But we use salt too! It's essential to bring out the flavors in food. We use it thoughtfully, not salting cooking water for pasta and vegetables all the time. When we use butter, it's unsalted. When you cook at home, consider seasoning dishes just before serving and using large-flake kosher or coarse sea salt. Teaspoon for teaspoon, these may contain less sodium—and the large crystals add a pleasant crunch and a hit of salty flavor even when used sparingly. Consider upping your potassium intake too. The mineral—abundant in produce, including bananas, squash, beans and spinach—can actually lessen the negative health effects of a salty diet.

7 CONSIDER THE ENVIRONMENT

Eating clean is not only better for you, it's also better for the planet. The food we eat takes a surprising amount of natural resources to produce—including land, water and fuel. And it leaves a lot of pollution in its wake, on both a small and grand scale. On the grand-scale side: The carbon emissions that agriculture and food manufacturing create are major contributors to global warming and the acidification of our oceans. In fact, by some estimates, the global food system accounts for a third of all greenhouse gas emissions. And one of the biggest offenders is the meat industry. In addition to all the resources it takes to feed and care for the animals over their life span, cattle, goats and sheep have a particularly large carbon footprint because of the methane they release during digestion and through their manure. In fact, raising animals for their meat—including pigs and poultry—generates as much greenhouse gas as all the vehicles on the planet combined. Pretty shocking, right? And, the poop from these animals—while full of beneficial nutrients—leaches pollutants like metals, nitrogen, phosphorus and antibiotics (in the case of conventionally raised animals) into our rivers, lakes and oceans.

Before you think this is some kind of anti-meat manifesto, meat isn't the only problem here of course. Modern fishing techniques have led to much bigger catches, resulting in overfishing of many species of seafood to the point of near extinction, as well as destruction of natural ocean habitats. And back on land, the herbicides, pesticides and synthetic fertilizers used to grow conventional produce have their own negative impacts on soil and water quality.

So how can eating clean help? Because going heavy on the veg and lighter on the meat can go a long way toward preserving Earth's natural resources, slowing, halting—and even reversing—the environmental damage being done. A study at Loma Linda University, for example, found that a vegetarian diet requires 3 times less water, 2.5 times less energy, 13 times less fertilizer and nearly 1.5 times less pesticide than a meat-heavy diet.

That's because the environmental impact of growing apples, zucchini or a field of wheat is significantly less than that of raising animals for their meat. Broccoli, for example, has an estimated carbon footprint that's *13 times* lower than that of the same amount of conventionally raised beef. (And supply follows demand—so if fewer people want porterhouses and chicken breasts, the number of animals being raised will decrease too.) Research published in the journal *Nature* found that shifting from a meat-forward way of eating to a more plant-based one could slash

---

MYTH OR TRUTH?
GMOS are bad for you.

Myth. While there has been some research linking genetically engineered foods with adverse health effects, a recent report from the National Academy of Sciences—which reviewed more than 900 studies on GMOs—found they actually don't pose any risk for conditions such as cancer, allergies and gastrointestinal issues. Still, GMOs are relatively new—they've only been used since the 1990s—and some people continue to worry about the possible long-term effects. One thing the report found GMOs *can* impact? The environment. Plants are often genetically engineered to withstand herbicides—allowing farmers to spray herbicides to kill weeds without harming the crops themselves. But that's led to so-called superweeds, and now farmers are seeking approval to use even stronger herbicides. If the idea of genetically altered foods makes you nervous, choose organic versions of them—particularly those containing corn and soybeans, nearly all of which are genetically engineered—or look for the non-GMO seal on conventional packaged goods.

greenhouse gas emissions—as well as add about a decade to your life.

According to the study, following these principles of clean eating could stave off the huge rise in greenhouse gas emissions and habitat destruction that's predicted if we continue to eat the diet we do today (lots of meat, processed foods and very little fruits and veg). In fact, the researchers estimated that if everyone started eating a cleaner, veg-heavy diet, in around 40 years global greenhouse gas emissions would be reduced by an amount equivalent to the total emissions of every car, truck, plane, train and ship on Earth.

Going organic on the occasions when you do eat meat is also a more environmentally sound choice. According to an EWG study, meat, eggs and dairy products that are certified organic or grass-fed have been found to be the least damaging. Part of that has to do with the fact that when cows and other free-range animals like chickens are regularly moved to fresh pasture, manure is spread more evenly, boosting the quality and quantity of pasture grasses, which in turn reduces soil erosion and water pollution. Ultimately, healthier soil and grasses also help to sequester more carbon in the ground, getting it out of the atmosphere. And when it comes to seafood, in addition to choosing low-mercury varieties for health reasons, you can double down on the do-gooding by also choosing fish and shellfish that have healthy wild populations or are farmed sustainably (*see Buyer's Guide, page 252*).

Finally, let's talk about all that amazing produce you're going to be eating. While fruits, veggies and legumes have a fairly small carbon footprint, you can make it even smaller by buying organic food. Organic farming methods eliminate the use of synthetic fertilizers and pesticides so they don't get into the soil and water supply, as well as into your body. Better yet, look for organic food that's local and in season—that way it doesn't have to travel so far to get to you.

MYTH OR TRUTH?

Canola oil is toxic.

Myth. It's true that 95 percent of canola in the United States is genetically engineered. So if that's something you'd rather avoid, just opt for certified organic or non-GMO. You may have also read that canola contains high levels of erucic acid—a compound that's toxic to humans. Though that was true years ago, it's long since been bred out of the canola plant we get our oil from today, and levels are low enough not to be harmful at all. Then there's talk about canola oil being processed using dangerous chemicals. The fact is, *all* oils are processed, in similar ways (yes, even expeller-pressed), and there's no good evidence to suggest the refining method is bad for you. OK, so what about partially hydrogenated oils—doesn't canola oil have these unhealthy trans fats? Sometimes, yes. But only in canola oil in solid form, which you'll find in certain spreads and baked goods. (The hydrogenation process makes the normally liquid oil a solid at room temperature.) Liquid canola oil, however, *does not* contain trans fats. In fact, liquid canola oil is chock-full of heart-healthy unsaturated fat and has a neutral taste—both reasons why we use it in recipes. There is some truth to the idea that cooking with canola oil can create a harmful compound, called HNE, which some research has linked to heart and liver disease, stroke and neurological problems like Parkinson's and Huntington's disease. Avoid it by making sure you don't heat the oil to its smoke point—which is when those toxins are made. In fact, when *any* oil—not just canola—is heated to its smoking point (or reused repeatedly), harmful compounds can form.

dinner in 20

Even when your day is hectic, you still want to find a way to make a fresh, delicious meal. The easy-to-prepare entrees in this chapter use only a handful of well-chosen ingredients, layering in plenty of fresh veggies with quick-cooking (or already-cooked) protein. Getting meals from kitchen to table fast doesn't mean resorting to highly processed shortcuts. Instead, we use tried-and-true techniques that save time, such as sautéing on the stovetop instead of waiting for the oven to heat up. And don't think that because a meal is quick, it has to be boring. We'll show you how to use just a few herbs and spices to add pops of flavor, and fresh citrus or vinegar to round out the seasoning of each of these dishes. Cooking quickly from scratch on a weeknight? Yup.

Smoked Mozzarella & Tomato Sandwiches
with Tapenade (*page 24*)

To Make Ahead: Prepare tapenade (Steps 1-3) and refrigerate for up to 4 days.

smoked mozzarella & tomato sandwiches
with tapenade

It's worth seeking out smoked mozzarella for these sandwiches as it adds a deep, nutty flavor you won't find in its fresh counterpart. Look for it in a well-stocked cheese section at larger markets and specialty cheese shops. *(Photo: page 22.)*

²/₃ cup sun-dried tomatoes (not packed in oil)

1 clove garlic, crushed and peeled

¹/₄ teaspoon salt

2 tablespoons extra-virgin olive oil, divided

1 tablespoon lemon juice

¹/₈ teaspoon crushed red pepper

2 tablespoons chopped pitted black olives

8 slices whole-wheat sourdough bread

4 ounces fresh mozzarella cheese, preferably smoked, cut into ¹/₄-inch-thick slices

Ground pepper to taste

3 ripe tomatoes, sliced

2 teaspoons balsamic vinegar

1 cup fresh basil leaves

1. Place sun-dried tomatoes in a bowl and cover with boiling water. Let plump for 10 minutes.

2. Mash garlic and salt into a paste with a chef's knife. Transfer to a bowl and whisk in 1 table-spoon oil, lemon juice and crushed red pepper.

3. Drain the sun-dried tomatoes and finely chop. Add to the garlic mixture along with olives and mix well.

4. Spread the tapenade on 4 slices of bread. Layer cheese on the tapenade and season with pepper. Add tomato slices, a drizzle of vinegar and several basil leaves. Brush the other 4 slices of bread with the remaining 1 tablespoon oil and place on top of the sandwiches.

SERVES 4: 1 sandwich each

Calories 417 | **Fat** 15g (sat 5g) | **Cholesterol** 22mg | **Carbohydrates** 50g | **Total sugars** 5g (added 0g) | **Protein** 15g | **Fiber** 5g | **Sodium** 785mg | **Potassium** 293mg. **Nutrition bonus:** Vitamin A (38% daily value) | Vitamin C (30% dv) | Calcium (20% dv).

creamy buffalo chicken salad

Nonfat Greek yogurt replaces more than half of the mayonnaise in this Buffalo-wing-inspired chicken salad. We like the flavor of Frank's RedHot sauce, but Tabasco is a delicious option too. Serve as an open-face sandwich or on top of salad greens.

$^1/_2$ cup nonfat plain **Greek yogurt**

$^1/_3$ cup **mayonnaise**

2 tablespoons minced **shallot**

2 tablespoons **hot sauce**, such as Frank's RedHot

2 teaspoons **lemon juice**

$^1/_2$ teaspoon **salt**

$^1/_2$ teaspoon **ground pepper**

3 cups shredded *or* chopped **cooked chicken** *(see Tip, page 247)*

$^3/_4$ cup chopped **celery**

$^3/_4$ cup chopped **carrots**

3 tablespoons crumbled **blue cheese**

Combine yogurt, mayonnaise, shallot, hot sauce, lemon juice, salt and pepper in a large bowl. Stir in chicken, celery and carrots. Top with blue cheese. Serve at room temperature or refrigerate until cold, about 2 hours.

SERVES 6: $^3/_4$ cup each

Calories 175 | Fat 12g (sat 3g) | Cholesterol 34mg | Carbohydrates 4g | Total sugars 2g (added 0g) | Protein 12g | Fiber 1g | Sodium 551mg | Potassium 222mg. Nutrition bonus: Vitamin A (55% daily value).

sicilian olive chicken

This saucy one-skillet chicken dinner is old-world rustic but quick. If you can't find cutlets, make your own by pounding trimmed halved chicken breasts with a meat mallet until flattened to about 1/2 inch thick. If you like, try black Cerignola olives in place of the green Sicilians or a combo of both. Serve over whole-wheat egg noodles with a mixed green salad.

1 **14-ounce can petite-diced tomatoes with garlic and olive oil** *or* **other Italian-style seasoning** *(see Tip)*

1 1/2 **cups frozen chopped spinach, thawed**

1/3 **cup halved pitted Sicilian** *or* **other green olives**

1 **tablespoon capers, rinsed**

1/4 **teaspoon crushed red pepper, or to taste**

4 **4-ounce chicken cutlets**

1/4 **teaspoon ground pepper**

1 **tablespoon extra-virgin olive oil**

1. Combine tomatoes, spinach, olives, capers and crushed red pepper in a bowl. Sprinkle both sides of chicken with pepper.

2. Heat oil in a large skillet over medium-high heat. Cook the chicken until browned on one side, 2 to 4 minutes. Turn and top the chicken with the tomato mixture. Reduce heat to medium, cover and cook until the chicken is cooked through, 3 to 5 minutes.

SERVES 4: 1 cutlet each

Calories 213 | **Fat** 8g (sat 2g) | **Cholesterol** 63mg | **Carbohydrates** 9g | **Total sugars** 4g (added 0g) | **Protein** 26g | **Fiber** 3g | **Sodium** 542mg | **Potassium** 606mg. **Nutrition bonus:** Vitamin A (143% daily value) | Folate (23% dv).

clean it up

Canned, boxed and jarred tomatoes boast a short list of ingredients. Two common additives may sound scary, but aren't. Citric acid is used to prevent the growth of microbes. It occurs naturally in foods like citrus and berries and is also synthetically made. According to the Center for Science in the Public Interest (CSPI), it's safe. Calcium chloride is simply a common electrolyte often used to help keep tomatoes firm. Note that some can linings still contain bisphenol A, a chemical that can be a hormone disruptor and present additional health risks. Choosing foods in cartons (Tetra Pak) or jars instead of cans can help limit your exposure.

seared salmon
with green peppercorn sauce

Green peppercorns come from the same plant as black ones, but are harvested before they mature. Typically packed in vinegar, they have a refreshingly sharp flavor. Look for them near the capers in most supermarkets. Serve with smashed red potatoes and sautéed kale.

1¼ **pounds wild salmon fillet** *(see Tip)*, **skinned** *(see Tip, page 247)* **and cut into 4 portions**

¼ **teaspoon salt plus a pinch, divided**

2 **teaspoons canola oil**

¼ **cup lemon juice**

4 **teaspoons unsalted butter, cut into small pieces**

1 **teaspoon green peppercorns in vinegar, rinsed and crushed**

Sprinkle salmon with ¼ teaspoon salt. Heat oil in a large nonstick skillet over medium-high heat. Add the salmon and cook until just opaque in the center, gently turning halfway, 4 to 7 minutes total. Divide among 4 plates. Remove the pan from the heat and immediately add lemon juice, butter, peppercorns and the remaining pinch of salt; swirl the pan carefully to incorporate the butter into the sauce. Top each portion of fish with sauce.

SERVES 4: 4 oz. salmon & about 2 tsp. sauce each

Calories 226 | **Fat** 11g (sat 4g) | **Cholesterol** 76mg | **Carbohydrates** 1g | **Total sugars** 0g (added 0g) | **Protein** 28g | **Fiber** 0g | **Sodium** 269mg | **Potassium** 543mg. **Nutrition bonus:** Vitamin B_{12} (101% daily value).

clean it up

Most wild salmon—and some farmed—is currently considered a sustainable choice. For farmed, ask for fish that's raised in land- or tank-based systems. For more information about sustainable seafood, go to *seafoodwatch.org*.

ACTIVE | 15 min
TOTAL | 15 min

To Make Ahead:
Refrigerate leftover
dressing for up to 3 days.

green goddess salad
with chicken

This easy salad is packed with crunchy romaine, snappy cucumber, sweet cherry tomatoes, creamy Swiss cheese and protein-rich chicken breast. The herb-flecked green goddess dressing gets its rich and creamy texture from avocado and buttermilk. Any extra dressing is terrific over grilled chicken or fish, such as cod or flounder.

DRESSING

1 ripe avocado, pitted and peeled

1½ cups buttermilk

¼ cup chopped fresh herbs (such as tarragon, sorrel, mint, parsley *and/or* cilantro)

2 tablespoons rice vinegar

½ teaspoon salt

SALAD

12 cups chopped romaine lettuce

4 cups sliced cucumber (2 medium)

3 cups sliced *or* diced cooked chicken (see *Tip, page 247*)

2 cups diced low-fat Swiss cheese (8 ounces)

4 cups cherry tomatoes, halved if desired

1. **To prepare dressing:** Place avocado, buttermilk, herbs, vinegar and salt in a blender and puree until smooth. (*Makes about 1¾ cups dressing.*)

2. **To prepare salad:** Divide lettuce and cucumber among 4 plates. Top each portion with some chicken, cheese and tomatoes. Drizzle each with 1 tablespoon of the dressing. (*Refrigerate the remaining dressing for up to 3 days.*)

SERVES 4: about 5 cups salad & 1 Tbsp. dressing each

Calories 283 | Fat 7g (sat 3g) | **Cholesterol** 70mg | **Carbohydrates** 15g | **Total sugars** 8g (added 0g) | **Protein** 40g | **Fiber** 6g | **Sodium** 245mg | **Potassium** 1,009mg. **Nutrition bonus:** Vitamin A (267% daily value) | Calcium (72% dv) | Folate (59% dv) | Vitamin C (41% dv) | Vitamin B_{12} (22% dv).

linguine with
creamy white clam sauce

Ripe tomato and fragrant basil freshen up this classic pasta dish made with clams, garlic and lemon juice. A scant amount of cream finishes the dish. Fresh or frozen chopped clams from the seafood department are the best option, as they have a higher clam-to-liquid ratio and are lower in sodium. If you do use canned, opt for whole baby clams for the best texture. Serve with crusty garlic bread and steamed green beans.

8 ounces whole-wheat linguine *(see Tip)*

1 16-ounce container chopped clams (thawed if frozen) *or* two 10-ounce cans whole baby clams

3 tablespoons extra-virgin olive oil

3 cloves garlic, chopped

1/4 teaspoon crushed red pepper

1 tablespoon lemon juice

1/4 teaspoon salt

1 large tomato, chopped

1/4 cup chopped fresh basil, plus more for garnish

2 tablespoons heavy cream *or* half-and-half

1. Bring a large saucepan of water to a boil. Add pasta and cook until just tender, about 8 minutes or according to package directions. Drain.

2. Meanwhile, drain clams, reserving 3/4 cup of the liquid. Heat oil in a large skillet over medium-high heat. Add garlic and crushed red pepper and cook, stirring, for 30 seconds. Add the reserved clam liquid, lemon juice and salt; bring to a simmer and cook until slightly reduced, 2 to 3 minutes. Add tomato and the clams; bring to a simmer and cook for 1 minute more. Remove from heat.

3. Stir in basil and cream (or half-and-half). Add the pasta and toss to coat with the sauce. Garnish with more basil, if desired.

SERVES 4: 1¹/4 cups each

Calories 382 | Fat 15g (sat 3g) | **Cholesterol** 50mg | **Carbohydrates** 46g | **Total sugars** 4g (added 0g) | **Protein** 20g | **Fiber** 9g | **Sodium** 371mg | **Potassium** 205mg. **Nutrition bonus:** Iron (22% daily value).

 *clean it up*

Whole-wheat pasta is rich in good-for-practically-everything fiber. But don't confuse it with enriched wheat-flour pasta, which is made from refined wheat flour that's been stripped of the nutritious bran and germ but had vitamins and minerals added back. Look for "whole-grain flour" or "whole-wheat flour" as the first ingredient.

veg-packed vegetarian

Choosing to eat less meat, even if only a few times a week, has great health benefits. But think about this: going vegetarian is also a fantastic way to add more excitement to your meals. Rather than choosing from just meat, poultry or fish to star in dishes, you can explore the hundreds of varieties of vegetables bursting with unique flavors, textures and colors. In this chapter we offer you vegetarian dishes from around the globe, like a filling Mexican *posole* featuring golden butternut squash *(page 43)* and peanut noodles studded with veggies and cubes of satisfying roasted tofu *(page 44)*. For those who crave a "meaty" bite, there's a crispy portobello "cutlet" with steakhouse-style toppings of caramelized onions and blue cheese *(page 51)*.

Greek Salad with Edamame *(page 34)*

creamy fettuccine
with brussels sprouts & mushrooms

Think of this creamy pasta dish as a fall version of pasta primavera. Choose presliced mushrooms and shredded Brussels sprouts at the supermarket to cut prep time. Serve with a green salad.

12 ounces whole-wheat fettuccine

1 tablespoon extra-virgin olive oil

4 cups sliced mixed mushrooms, such as cremini, oyster *and/or* shiitake

4 cups thinly sliced Brussels sprouts

1 tablespoon minced garlic

$1/2$ cup dry sherry *(see Tip) or* 2 tablespoons sherry vinegar

2 cups low-fat milk

2 tablespoons white whole-wheat flour

$1/2$ teaspoon salt

$1/2$ teaspoon ground pepper

1 cup finely grated Asiago cheese, plus more for garnish

clean it up

Opt for a real bottle of wine, even an inexpensive one, over bottled cooking wine. Cooking wine contains loads of added sodium (about 200 mg per ounce, on average) that doesn't need to end up in your meal. If you're worried about wasting the rest of the bottle, freeze extra wine in ice cube trays to use another time.

1. Bring a large saucepan of water to a boil. Add pasta and cook until just tender, 8 to 10 minutes or according to package directions. Drain and return to the pot.

2. Meanwhile, heat oil in a large skillet over medium heat. Add mushrooms and Brussels sprouts and cook, stirring often, until the mushrooms release their liquid, 8 to 10 minutes. Add garlic and cook, stirring, until fragrant, about 1 minute. Stir in sherry (or vinegar), scraping up any browned bits. Bring to a boil and cook, stirring, until almost evaporated, 10 seconds (if using vinegar) or about 1 minute (if using sherry).

3. Whisk milk and flour in a bowl; add to the skillet. Season with salt and pepper. Cook, stirring, until the sauce bubbles and thickens, about 2 minutes. Stir in cheese until melted. Add the sauce to the pasta and gently toss. Serve with more cheese, if desired.

SERVES 6: about $1^1/3$ cups each

Calories 383 | **Fat** 10g (sat 4g) | **Cholesterol** 21mg | **Carbohydrates** 56g | **Total sugars** 8g (added 0g) | **Protein** 19g | **Fiber** 10g | **Sodium** 431mg | **Potassium** 598mg. **Nutrition bonus:** Vitamin C (75% daily value) | Calcium (29% dv).

ACTIVE 45 min
TOTAL 45 min

To Make Ahead:
Prepare filling (Step 3) and
refrigerate for up to 1 day.

vegetarian shepherd's pies

Individual shepherd's pies are a cinch to throw together and make the ideal comfort food for a chilly evening. The recipe can also be made family-style in a 2-quart broiler-safe baking dish.

1 **pound Yukon Gold *or* white potatoes, peeled and cut into 1-inch chunks**

1/2 **cup buttermilk**

1 **tablespoon butter**

3/4 **teaspoon salt, divided**

1/2 **teaspoon ground pepper, divided**

1 **tablespoon extra-virgin olive oil**

1 **large onion, finely diced**

1/2 **cup finely diced carrot**

1 **tablespoon water**

3/4 **cup frozen corn kernels, thawed**

1 **teaspoon chopped fresh thyme *or* 1/2 teaspoon dried**

3 **tablespoons white whole-wheat flour**

1 **14-ounce can vegetable broth**

1 1/2 **cups cooked *or* canned (rinsed) lentils (see Tip, page 247)**

1. Place potatoes in a large saucepan and cover with 2 inches of water. Bring to a simmer over medium-high heat. Reduce heat to medium, partially cover and cook until tender, 10 to 15 minutes. Drain and return to the pot. Add buttermilk, butter and 1/4 teaspoon each salt and pepper. Mash until mostly smooth.

2. Meanwhile, position a rack in upper third of oven and preheat broiler. Coat four 10- to 12-ounce broiler-safe ramekins (or an 8-inch-square broiler-safe baking dish) with cooking spray and place on a baking sheet.

3. Heat oil in a large skillet over medium-high heat. Add onion, carrot and water. Cover and cook, stirring occasionally, until softened, 3 to 5 minutes. Stir in corn, thyme and the remaining 1/2 teaspoon salt and 1/4 teaspoon pepper; cook, stirring occasionally, for 2 minutes. Sprinkle with flour and stir to coat. Stir in broth. Bring to a simmer; cook, stirring, for 1 minute. Stir in lentils and cook, stirring constantly, for 2 minutes.

4. Divide the lentil mixture among the prepared ramekins (or spread in the baking dish). Top with the mashed potatoes. Broil, rotating halfway through, until the potato is lightly browned in spots, 6 to 10 minutes.

SERVES 4: about 2 cups each

Calories 319 | Fat 7g (sat 3g) | Cholesterol 9mg | Carbohydrates 54g | Total sugars 8g (added 0g) | Protein 12g | Fiber 10g | Sodium 783mg | Potassium 844mg. Nutrition bonus: Vitamin A (57% daily value) | Folate (41% dv) | Vitamin C (25% dv).

ACTIVE 40 min
TOTAL 40 min

tofu & vegetable stew

Miso, a fermented soybean paste, and seaweed are both umami ingredients that give this stew a wonderful meaty richness. (Dulse and arame, two of the most common seaweeds used in Asian cooking, can be found in Asian or natural-foods markets.) The addition of eggs, tofu, sweet corn kernels and cabbage results in a well-rounded meal. Use firm silken tofu if you prefer a soft texture; opt for regular firm tofu for more chewiness.

1½ tablespoons canola oil

1 medium onion, chopped

1½ tablespoons grated *or* minced fresh ginger

4 cups thinly sliced napa cabbage

4 cups vegetable broth

½ cup snipped dulse *or* arame seaweed

1 cup corn kernels, fresh *or* frozen

2 12- to 14-ounce packages firm tofu *(see Tip)*, silken *or* regular, drained if necessary, cut into ¼-inch cubes

¼ cup white miso

2 large eggs, beaten

4 scallions, chopped

2 tablespoons rice vinegar

1. Heat oil in a large pot over medium-high heat. Add onion and ginger; cook, stirring often, until fragrant, about 1 minute. Add cabbage; cook, stirring occasionally, until starting to wilt, 1 to 2 minutes.

2. Add broth and seaweed; bring to a boil. Reduce heat to medium and simmer for 5 minutes. Add corn, return to a simmer and cook for 2 minutes. Add tofu and cook until hot, about 3 minutes. Stir in miso and cook for 1 minute more.

3. Drizzle eggs onto the surface of the stew and simmer, undisturbed, until just set, 1 to 2 minutes. Remove from heat. Add scallions and vinegar and gently stir to combine.

SERVES 5: about 2 cups each

Calories 239 | Fat 11g (sat 2g) | Cholesterol 74mg | Carbohydrates 20g | Total sugars 8g (added 0g) | Protein 16g | Fiber 4g | Sodium 731mg | Potassium 606mg. Nutrition bonus: Vitamin C (26% daily value).

clean it up

Tofu is made from soybean milk, and coagulant helps to solidify it and keep its form. The most commonly used coagulants are magnesium chloride, calcium sulfate, calcium chloride and nigari (evaporated seawater with the sodium removed). These coagulants are not only safe, according to the FDA and the Center for Science in the Public Interest (CSPI), but also add nutritional value via the minerals calcium or magnesium (depending on which coagulant is used).

butternut squash & tomato posole

Posole is a traditional Mexican stew that is most often made with pork and hominy (dried corn kernels that have been treated to soften the hull) cooked in a fragrant chile-based sauce. In this quick vegetarian version, the meatiness of pinto beans and squash combined with hand-crushed whole tomatoes make it satisfying. Look for butternut squash that is already peeled and cubed in the produce department of most supermarkets to speed things up.

1 **28-ounce can whole peeled tomatoes, preferably no-salt-added**

1 **tablespoon canola oil**

2 **cups chopped red onion**

4 **cloves garlic, minced**

2 **tablespoons chili powder**

3 **cups diced (1/2-inch) peeled butternut squash**

1½ **cups vegetable broth**

1 **15-ounce can white hominy, rinsed**

1 **15-ounce can pinto beans, rinsed** *(see Tip)*

1 **firm ripe avocado, diced**

1/4 **cup chopped fresh cilantro**

1. Working over a bowl, break apart tomatoes with your fingers one at a time, letting them drop into the bowl. Reserve the juice.

2. Heat oil in a large pot over medium-high heat. Add onion and garlic and cook, stirring often, until beginning to brown, 4 to 5 minutes. Add chili powder and cook, stirring, for 30 seconds. Add squash, broth, hominy, beans, the crushed tomatoes and their juice. Bring to a simmer. Reduce heat to maintain a gentle simmer.

3. Cover and cook, stirring occasionally, until the squash is tender, 25 to 30 minutes. Serve topped with avocado and cilantro.

SERVES 5: about 1²/₃ cups each

Calories 306 | Fat 10g (sat 1g) | Cholesterol 0mg | Carbohydrates 51g | Total sugars 12g (added 0g) | Protein 8g | Fiber 16g | Sodium 496mg | Potassium 1,232mg. Nutrition bonus: Vitamin A (302% daily value) | Vitamin C (67% dv) | Folate (27% dv).

 *clean it up*

Rinse your canned beans well and you can remove up to 35 percent of the sodium reported on the label. If you're looking to cut even more sodium, choose canned beans with no added salt.

roasted tofu & peanut noodle salad

Peanut butter adds richness, flavor and protein to this light noodle dish. And making this takeout favorite at home means you can keep it clean without added sugar. Cabbage, bell pepper and snow peas add color and crunch, but try other veggies like sugar snap peas or carrots if you like. For added crunch, top it off with chopped roasted peanuts.

¹/₄ cup lime juice

¹/₄ cup reduced-sodium soy sauce

1 tablespoon canola oil

1 14- to 16-ounce package extra-firm water-packed tofu, cut into ¹/₂-inch cubes

6 ounces whole-wheat spaghetti

¹/₂ cup smooth natural peanut butter *(see Tip, opposite)*

3 tablespoons water

3 cloves garlic, minced

1 tablespoon minced fresh ginger

6 cups thinly sliced napa cabbage

1 medium orange bell pepper, thinly sliced

1 cup thinly sliced trimmed snow peas

1. Position rack in lower third of oven; preheat to 450°F. Coat a large baking sheet with cooking spray. Put a large pot of water on to boil for spaghetti.

2. Combine lime juice, soy sauce and oil in a large bowl. Stir in tofu; marinate, stirring frequently, for 10 minutes.

3. Using a slotted spoon, transfer the tofu to the prepared baking sheet. (Reserve the marinade.) Roast the tofu, stirring once halfway through, until golden brown, 16 to 18 minutes.

4. Meanwhile, cook spaghetti according to package directions. Drain.

5. Whisk peanut butter, water, garlic and ginger into the reserved marinade. Add the cooked spaghetti, cabbage, bell pepper and snow peas; toss to coat. Serve topped with the tofu.

SERVES 5: 2 cups each

Calories 425 | Fat 21g (sat 3g) | Cholesterol 0mg | Carbohydrates 40g | Total sugars 5g (added 0g) | Protein 21g | Fiber 9g | Sodium 531mg | Potassium 522mg. Nutrition bonus: Vitamin C (108% daily value) | Vitamin A (39% dv) | Folate (26% dv) | Calcium & Iron (22% dv).

🍎 clean it up

Want the best peanut butter? The only ingredients you should see on the ingredient list are peanuts and salt. Avoid varieties with added oils and sweeteners, often labeled "no stir" or "peanut spread." "Peanut spread" means it contains less than 90 percent peanuts. And skip the low-fat varieties—the fat is usually replaced with added sugar.

ACTIVE | 40 min

TOTAL | 40 min

To Make Ahead: Refrigerate roasted tofu and chickpeas (Steps 1-3) for up to 2 days.

kale salad
with spiced tofu & chickpeas

Cumin, paprika and lemon juice add flavor to the roasted tofu and chickpeas as well as the dressing for this raw kale salad. Roasting the tofu and chickpeas in a hot oven leaves them crisp on the outside and creamy on the inside.

3 1/2 teaspoons ground cumin

3 1/2 teaspoons paprika

2 teaspoons garlic powder

1 teaspoon ground pepper

3/4 teaspoon salt

5 tablespoons lemon juice, divided

4 tablespoons extra-virgin olive oil, divided

1 14-ounce package extra-firm water-packed tofu, drained and cut into 3/4-inch cubes

1 15-ounce can chickpeas, rinsed

14 cups torn kale (from 1 large bunch) or baby kale

1 medium bell pepper, cut into 2-inch-long strips

1/2 English cucumber, halved and sliced

1. Position rack in lower third of oven; preheat to 450°F. Coat a large baking sheet with cooking spray.

2. Combine cumin, paprika, garlic powder, pepper and salt in a large bowl. Measure out 2 1/2 teaspoons and set aside. Add 2 tablespoons lemon juice and 1 tablespoon oil to the remaining spice mixture. Pat tofu dry. Add the tofu and chickpeas to the marinade and stir to combine; let stand for 10 minutes.

3. Spread the tofu and chickpeas in a single layer on the prepared baking sheet. Roast on the lower rack, stirring once halfway, until golden brown, about 20 minutes.

4. Meanwhile, return the reserved 2 1/2 teaspoons spice mixture to the bowl and whisk in the remaining 3 tablespoons each lemon juice and oil. Add kale and, with clean hands, massage until the greens are reduced in volume by almost half, 1 to 2 minutes. Add bell pepper and cucumber and toss to combine.

5. Serve the salad topped with the roasted tofu and chickpeas.

SERVES 4: 2 1/4 cups salad & 3/4 cup tofu mixture each

Calories 356 | **Fat** 20g (sat 3g) | **Cholesterol** 0mg | **Carbohydrates** 33g | **Total sugars** 4g (added 0g) | **Protein** 16g | **Fiber** 8g | **Sodium** 632mg | **Potassium** 781mg. **Nutrition bonus:** Vitamin C (223% daily value) | Vitamin A (134% dv) | Folate (42% dv) | Calcium (34% dv) | Iron (27% dv).

summer vegetable pasta
with crispy goat cheese medallions

This pasta is loaded with the best of early-summer vegetables—sweet spring onions, tangy cherry tomatoes and plenty of baby spinach. The crisped goat cheese medallions take just a minute or two under the broiler, yet add a nice touch.

- **8** ounces whole-wheat bow-tie pasta
- **1¹/₂** tablespoons chopped fresh dill
- **1¹/₂** tablespoons coarse dry whole-wheat breadcrumbs *(see Tip, page 247)*
- **4** ounces soft goat cheese
- Olive oil cooking spray
- **2** tablespoons extra-virgin olive oil
- **3** spring onion bulbs, halved and thinly sliced, or 2 cups thinly sliced small onions
- **1¹/₂** pints cherry tomatoes, halved (3 cups)
- **2** cloves garlic, sliced
- **¹/₂** teaspoon salt
- **¹/₄** teaspoon ground pepper
- **6** cups baby spinach

1. Position rack in upper third of oven; preheat broiler. Line a baking sheet with foil.

2. Bring a large saucepan of water to a boil. Cook pasta according to package directions. Reserve ¹/₂ cup of the cooking water, then drain.

3. Meanwhile, combine dill and breadcrumbs in a small bowl. Divide goat cheese into four 1-inch-diameter round medallions. Coat in the breadcrumb mixture, lightly patting the mixture onto the cheese to help it stick. Place on the prepared baking sheet and lightly coat the tops with cooking spray. Set aside.

4. Heat oil in a large skillet over medium heat. Add onions and cook, stirring, until lightly browned, 5 to 6 minutes. Add tomatoes, garlic, salt and pepper; cook until the tomatoes release their juice, 1 to 2 minutes. Stir in the reserved pasta-cooking water, scraping up any browned bits. Stir in spinach and the pasta; remove from heat.

5. Broil the goat cheese medallions, watching closely, until light brown and crispy on top, 1 to 2 minutes. Serve each portion of pasta topped with a goat cheese medallion.

SERVES 4: 1³/₄ cups each

Calories 394 | **Fat** 15g (sat 5g) | **Cholesterol** 13mg | **Carbohydrates** 53g | **Total sugars** 6g (added 0g) | **Protein** 17g | **Fiber** 8g | **Sodium** 493mg | **Potassium** 749mg. **Nutrition bonus:** Vitamin A (119% daily value) | Vitamin C (63% dv) | Folate (37% dv) | Iron (26% dv).

greek salad
with edamame

Edamame adds protein to the classic Greek salad: romaine, tomatoes, cucumber, feta and olives. Serve with toasted pita brushed with olive oil and sprinkled with dried oregano or za'atar. (*Photo: page 34.*)

¹/₄ **cup red-wine vinegar**

3 **tablespoons extra-virgin olive oil**

¹/₄ **teaspoon salt**

¹/₄ **teaspoon ground pepper**

8 **cups chopped romaine (about 2 romaine hearts)**

16 **ounces frozen shelled edamame (about 3 cups), thawed** (*see Tip*)

1 **cup halved cherry** *or* **grape tomatoes**

¹/₂ **European cucumber, sliced**

¹/₂ **cup crumbled feta cheese**

¹/₄ **cup slivered fresh basil**

¹/₄ **cup sliced Kalamata olives**

¹/₄ **cup slivered red onion**

1. Whisk vinegar, oil, salt and pepper in a large bowl.

2. Add romaine, edamame, tomatoes, cucumber, feta, basil, olives and onion; toss to coat.

SERVES 4: 2³/₄ cups each

Calories 344 | **Fat** 23g (sat 5g) | **Cholesterol** 17mg | **Carbohydrates** 20g | **Total sugars** 6g (added 0g) | **Protein** 17g | **Fiber** 9g | **Sodium** 489mg | **Potassium** 908mg. **Nutrition bonus:** Vitamin A (184% daily value) | Folate (125% dv) | Vitamin C (30% dv) | Iron (23% dv) | Calcium (22% dv).

clean it up

In 2016, 94 percent of U.S. soybeans were genetically modified. If you want to avoid GM foods, opt for organic soy products.

portobello cutlets
with caramelized onions & blue cheese

Here we give portobello mushroom cutlets the steakhouse treatment by searing them in a hot skillet until crisp and then topping them with caramelized onions and blue cheese. Serve the mushroom "steaks" with a baked potato and creamed spinach for the full effect.

$^1/_3$ cup balsamic vinegar

2 tablespoons reduced-sodium soy sauce

$^3/_4$ teaspoon dried sage

8 small portobello mushroom caps
(3-4 inches in diameter)

5 tablespoons extra-virgin olive oil, divided

2 cups sliced red onions

2 tablespoons water

$^1/_4$ teaspoon salt

$^1/_4$ teaspoon ground pepper

$^3/_4$ cup coarse dry whole-wheat breadcrumbs
(see Tip, page 247)

$^1/_4$ cup crumbled blue cheese

1. Combine vinegar, soy sauce and sage in a small bowl. Place mushroom caps, gill-side up, in a large shallow dish and pour the vinegar mixture into them. Let marinate for about 10 minutes.

2. Meanwhile, heat 1 tablespoon oil in a medium skillet over medium heat. Add onions and cook, stirring often, until just starting to brown, about 10 minutes. Add water and cook until the onions are very soft, 10 to 15 minutes more. Season with salt and pepper. Set aside.

3. Preheat oven to 250°F.

4. Place breadcrumbs on a large plate. Turn the mushrooms to coat on both sides with the marinade, then dredge them in the breadcrumbs.

5. Heat 1 tablespoon oil in a large nonstick skillet over medium heat. Add 4 mushrooms, gill-side down. Place a heavy, heatproof plate on top and cook until the breadcrumbs are browned, pressing on the plate periodically to flatten the mushrooms, about 4 minutes. Remove the plate; add 1 tablespoon oil to the pan and turn the mushrooms over. Replace the plate and cook, pressing once or twice, until the mushrooms are tender, about 4 minutes more. Transfer to a baking sheet and keep warm in the oven. Wipe out the pan and repeat with the remaining 4 mushrooms and 2 tablespoons oil, reducing the heat if necessary. Serve with the onions and blue cheese.

SERVES 4: 2 mushroom caps, 2 Tbsp. onions & 1 Tbsp. cheese each

Calories 341 | Fat 22g (sat 4g) | Cholesterol 6mg | Carbohydrates 28g | Total sugars 11g (added 1g) | Protein 10g | Fiber 5g | Sodium 580mg | Potassium 895mg. Nutrition bonus: Folate (20% daily value).

clean it up

Look for tostada shells made from whole-grain corn flour that don't contain palm oil or partially hydrogenated oils, which can have negative effects on heart health. Palm oil, an oil that—you guessed it—comes from palm trees, is high in saturated fat, which most experts agree can raise LDL "bad" cholesterol. It also contains a type of saturated fat, called palmitic acid, that could increase appetite. And finally, most harvesting for palm oil destroys rainforest habitat. Choose tostada shells that are baked or cooked in healthier oils, such as canola, safflower or sunflower oil. Or buy corn tortillas and make your own.

butternut squash & black bean tostadas

Ancho chile powder adds a mild, sweet-spicy flavor to the hearty squash-and-bean base of these vegetarian tostadas. Look for it in the spice section of well-stocked supermarkets. Other mildly spicy chili powder can be used in its place. Don't forget to put your arsenal of hot sauces on the table for drizzling.

1 **20-ounce package cubed peeled butternut squash** *or* **1 large butternut squash, peeled and cubed**

2 **teaspoons ancho chile powder, divided**

1/2 **teaspoon salt**

1 **15-ounce can black beans** *or* **pinto beans, rinsed**

2 **scallions, sliced**

3 **tablespoons lime juice, divided**

2 **tablespoons grapeseed** *or* **canola oil, divided**

1/2 **teaspoon ground cumin**

3 **cups chopped romaine lettuce**

8 **tostada shells** *(see Tip, opposite)*

1/2 **cup crumbled queso blanco** *or* **feta cheese**

1/4 **cup toasted unsalted pepitas** *(see Tip, page 247)*

1. Bring about 1 inch of water to a boil in a large saucepan fitted with a steamer basket. Add squash, cover and steam until very tender, about 15 minutes. Drain and return to the pan. Add 1½ teaspoons chile powder and salt. Mash until mostly smooth; cover to keep warm.

2. Meanwhile, combine beans, scallions, 2 tablespoons lime juice, 1 tablespoon oil, cumin and the remaining ½ teaspoon chile powder in a medium bowl. Toss lettuce with the remaining 1 tablespoon each lime juice and oil in another bowl.

3. Spread about ¼ cup squash on each tostada. Top each with about 3 tablespoons of the bean mixture, ¼ cup lettuce and 1 tablespoon cheese. Sprinkle with pepitas.

SERVES 4: 2 tostadas each

Calories 422 | Fat 21g (sat 5g) | Cholesterol 10mg | Carbohydrates 51g | Total sugars 8g (added 0g) | Protein 14g | Fiber 11g | Sodium 674mg | Potassium 1,019mg. Nutrition bonus: Vitamin A (374% daily value) | Vitamin C (64% dv) | Folate (36% dv) | Magnesium (32% dv) | Potassium (29% dv) | Calcium 25% dv) | Iron (24% dv).

great grains

Going the whole-grain route instead of refined is one of the simplest ways to get on the path to clean eating. In this chapter, we've pulled together our favorite grain-packed recipes to show that grains can be super versatile and—in spite of their reputation otherwise—quick as well. Some, like quinoa and bulgur, can be made in 15 minutes or less. And if you really want to be a master of convenience, cook a big batch ahead of time. Use as needed over the next few days or spread the cooked grains on a baking sheet (so they don't clump), freeze and then transfer to an airtight container so you're ready to go whole any night of the week. We feature toothsome farro in a creamy risotto-style dish, use red and wild rice as well as quinoa to amp up main-dish salads and even turn to rolled oats to take the place of grits in a playful rendition of shrimp and grits.

Cherry, Wild Rice & Quinoa Salad *(page 61)*

farrotto with artichokes

Farro (or emmer wheat) is a staple in central and northern Italy. Here, we've cooked farro in the style of risotto for a creamy, yet chewy, result. Plenty of herbs, garlic, tomatoes, artichokes and lemon zest give this dish amazing flavor.

1½ cups farro, rinsed

1 fresh sage leaf

1 sprig fresh rosemary

1 tablespoon extra-virgin olive oil

½ cup finely chopped onion

1 teaspoon finely chopped garlic

1 15-ounce can diced tomatoes, drained well

1 10-ounce box frozen artichoke hearts, thawed and coarsely chopped

¼ cup torn fresh basil

½ teaspoon coarse salt

Ground pepper to taste

Pinch of crushed red pepper

1½-2 cups reduced-sodium chicken broth, vegetable broth *or* water

½ cup grated Pecorino Romano cheese, divided

1 teaspoon lemon zest

1. Place farro in a large saucepan and cover with about 2 inches of water. Add sage and rosemary. Bring to a boil; reduce the heat and simmer until the farro is tender but still firm to the bite, 20 to 30 minutes. Remove the herbs and drain.

2. Heat oil in the pan over medium heat. Add onion and cook, stirring, until soft and beginning to brown, 3 to 5 minutes. Add garlic and cook, stirring, for 1 minute. Stir in the farro, tomatoes, artichokes, basil, salt, pepper and crushed red pepper.

3. Add ½ cup broth (or water), bring to a boil over medium heat and cook, stirring, until most of the liquid has been absorbed. Repeat with the remaining broth (or water), adding it in ½-cup increments and stirring until it has been absorbed before adding more, until the farro is creamy but still has a bit of bite, about 10 minutes total. Stir in ¼ cup cheese and lemon zest. Serve sprinkled with the remaining ¼ cup cheese.

SERVES 6: about 1 cup each

Calories 261 | Fat 6g (sat 2g) | Cholesterol 8mg | Carbohydrates 43g | Total sugars 4g (added 0g) | Protein 10g | Fiber 8g | Sodium 505mg | Potassium 283mg. Nutrition bonus: Folate (20% daily value).

roasted chicken & vegetable quinoa salad

Mushrooms, carrots and onions are roasted with garlic and fennel seeds for this salad. Preparing the quinoa with a little less water than is typical keeps it fluffier—perfect for soaking up the sherry-vinegar dressing.

3 cloves garlic, minced

1 teaspoon salt, divided

5 tablespoons extra-virgin olive oil

3 teaspoons fennel seeds, crushed, divided

$1/2$ teaspoon ground pepper, divided

10 ounces mushrooms, quartered

4 medium carrots, sliced $1/2$ inch thick

1 medium onion, cut into $3/4$-inch wedges

$1^1/2$ cups water

1 cup quinoa

1 pound chicken tenders, halved crosswise

3 tablespoons sherry vinegar *or* red-wine vinegar

8 cups torn escarole *or* curly endive

1. Preheat oven to 475°F.

2. Mash garlic and $3/4$ teaspoon salt into a paste with the side of a chef's knife or a fork. Transfer to a large bowl and whisk in oil, 2 teaspoons fennel seeds and $1/4$ teaspoon pepper.

3. Combine mushrooms, carrots and onion in a medium bowl. Drizzle with 2 tablespoons of the oil mixture and toss well to coat. Spread the vegetables on a large rimmed baking sheet. Roast for 10 minutes.

4. Meanwhile, combine water and quinoa in a medium saucepan; bring to a boil. Cover, reduce heat to maintain a simmer and cook for 10 minutes. Remove from heat, cover and set aside.

5. Toss chicken with 2 teaspoons of the oil mixture, the remaining 1 teaspoon fennel seeds and $1/4$ teaspoon each salt and pepper in the medium bowl.

6. Stir the vegetables and nestle the chicken among them. Roast until an instant-read thermometer inserted into the thickest part of a chicken tender registers 165°F, 8 to 10 minutes more.

7. Whisk vinegar into the remaining oil mixture. Add escarole (or endive) and the quinoa and toss with the dressing. Serve the salad topped with the roasted vegetables and chicken.

SERVES 4: about $2^1/4$ cups each

Calories 516 | Fat 24g (sat 4g) | Cholesterol 63mg | Carbohydrates 43g | Total sugars 8g (added 0g) | Protein 34g | Fiber 10g | Sodium 711mg | Potassium 1,242mg. Nutrition bonus: Vitamin A (248% daily value) | Folate (63% dv) | Iron (25% dv) | Vitamin C (24% dv).

ACTIVE : 35 min
TOTAL : 35 min

beef & bulgur burgers
with blue cheese

Bulgur is a great weeknight whole grain because it's been partially cooked before being dried. Check the package directions—some brands just need a quick soak in boiling water, while others need to be cooked for up to 15 minutes. Serve with roasted potato wedges and sliced tomatoes.

$^1/_2$ cup bulgur

1 cup sliced red onion

$^1/_2$ cup water

$^1/_2$ cup red-wine vinegar

1 pound 90%-lean ground beef

$^1/_2$ cup crumbled blue cheese

$^1/_2$ teaspoon celery salt *or* $^1/_4$ teaspoon salt

$^1/_2$ teaspoon ground pepper

1 tablespoon extra-virgin olive oil

4 large pieces green-leaf lettuce

1. Prepare bulgur according to package directions. Drain in a fine-mesh sieve, pressing to extract as much liquid as possible. Transfer to a large bowl. Let cool for 5 minutes.

2. Meanwhile, combine onion, water and vinegar in a medium saucepan. Bring to a boil and cook for 2 minutes. Remove from heat and set aside, stirring occasionally.

3. Add beef, blue cheese, celery salt (or salt) and pepper to the bulgur; use your hands to gently combine. Form the mixture into 4 burgers, about 4 inches in diameter.

4. Heat oil in a large nonstick skillet over medium heat. Cook the burgers until browned and an instant-read thermometer inserted into the thickest part registers 165°F, 4 to 6 minutes per side. Drain the pickled onion. Serve each burger on a lettuce leaf, topped with onion.

SERVES 4: 1 burger & $^1/_4$ cup onion each

Calories 344 | Fat 18g (sat 7g) | Cholesterol 85mg | Carbohydrates 17 g | Total sugars 2g (added 0g) | Protein 28g | Fiber 3g | Sodium 380mg | Potassium 472mg. Nutrition bonus: Vitamin B_{12} (38% daily value).

cherry, wild rice & quinoa salad

This salad is perfect for toting to summer potlucks. It features sweet cherries, crunchy celery, nutty aged goat cheese and toasted pecans. Using red quinoa makes the dish particularly pretty. Cut down on overall cooking time by using quick-cooking wild rice. *(Photo: page 54.)*

¾ **cup wild rice**

½ **cup quinoa**

¼ **cup extra-virgin olive oil**

¼ **cup fruity vinegar, such as raspberry** *or* **pomegranate** *(see Tip)*

¾ **teaspoon salt**

¼ **teaspoon ground pepper**

2 **cups halved pitted fresh sweet cherries** *(see Tip, page 247)*

2 **stalks celery, diced**

¾ **cup diced aged goat cheese** *or* **smoked Cheddar**

½ **cup chopped pecans, toasted** *(see Tip, page 247)*

1. Bring a large saucepan of water to a boil over high heat. Add wild rice and cook for 30 minutes. Add quinoa and cook until the rice and quinoa are tender, about 15 minutes more. Drain and rinse with cold water until cool to the touch; drain well.

2. Meanwhile, whisk oil, vinegar, salt and pepper in a large bowl. Add the rice and quinoa, cherries, celery, cheese and pecans and toss to combine. Serve at room temperature or cold.

SERVES 8: about ¾ cup each

Calories 282 | Fat 16g (sat 4g) | Cholesterol 10mg | Carbohydrates 27g | Total sugars 7g (added 0g) | Protein 8g | Fiber 3g | Sodium 272mg | Potassium 265mg.

clean it up

Flavored vinegars may contain "natural flavors," which come from a natural source like a plant, insect or animal. The FDA says they're safe to consume, but their sources—like bugs—can have an ick-factor. Some are genetically modified (GM). Companies often don't disclose the origin of natural flavorings on the ingredient list, so if you want to avoid them, choose a vinegar without them.

two-pepper shrimp
with creamy pecorino oats

Oats are not just for breakfast! In this rendition of shrimp and grits, we simmer oats with scallions and nutty aged cheese for a savory, creamy dish reminiscent of risotto. You'll even get your veggies with sautéed baby spinach on the side. Serve with your favorite hot sauce.

6 teaspoons extra-virgin olive oil, divided

3 teaspoons butter, divided

6 scallions, white and light green parts sliced, divided

1 cup old-fashioned rolled oats

2 cups water

$1/2$ teaspoon salt, divided

$1/2$ teaspoon ground pepper, divided

1 pound raw shrimp (16-20 count), peeled and deveined

$1/8$ teaspoon cayenne pepper, or to taste

1 pound baby spinach

$1/4$ teaspoon hot sauce, or to taste

$1/2$ cup grated Pecorino Romano *or* Parmesan cheese

1. Heat 2 teaspoons oil and 1 teaspoon butter in a medium saucepan over medium heat until the butter is melted. Add scallion whites and cook, stirring occasionally, until softened, 2 to 3 minutes. Add oats and cook, stirring, for 1 minute, then add water and $1/4$ teaspoon each salt and pepper. Bring to a boil. Reduce heat to maintain a simmer and cook, stirring often, until creamy, 8 to 10 minutes.

2. Meanwhile, sprinkle shrimp with cayenne and the remaining $1/4$ teaspoon pepper. Heat 1 tablespoon oil in a large skillet over medium-high heat. Add the shrimp and cook until just opaque, 2 to 4 minutes per side. Transfer to a clean bowl; cover to keep warm.

3. Add 1 teaspoon each oil and butter to the skillet. Add half the spinach; cook, stirring, until slightly wilted, about 1 minute. Add the remaining spinach and cook, stirring, until wilted, 2 to 3 minutes more. Add hot sauce and the remaining $1/4$ teaspoon salt.

4. Stir cheese and the remaining 1 teaspoon butter into the oats. Serve the oats with the spinach and shrimp. Sprinkle with the scallion greens.

SERVES 4: 4-5 shrimp, $1/2$ cup oats & $1/2$ cup spinach each

Calories 341 | **Fat** 15g (sat 5g) | **Cholesterol** 199mg | **Carbohydrates** 21g | **Total sugars** 2g (added 0g) | **Protein** 33g | **Fiber** 5g | **Sodium** 705mg | **Potassium** 1,020mg. **Nutrition bonus:** Vitamin A (221% daily value) | Folate (59% dv) | Vitamin C (60% dv) | Calcium (30% dv) | Iron (28% dv).

za'atar-roasted chicken tenders & vegetables
with couscous

Za'atar (or zaatar)—a Middle-Eastern spice blend that's a mix of thyme, sumac, salt, sesame seeds and sometimes other herbs—gives this sheet-pan chicken dinner tons of flavor. Chicken tenders and pretrimmed green beans keep this recipe especially quick.

1 medium navel orange
1 pound trimmed green beans
1 medium red onion, halved and sliced
1/2 cup Kalamata *or* Castelveltrano olives
2 tablespoons extra-virgin olive oil
2 tablespoons dry white wine
1/4 teaspoon salt
1/2 teaspoon ground pepper, divided
1 pound chicken tenders
1 tablespoon za'atar
1 cup low-sodium chicken broth
2/3 cup whole-wheat couscous

1. Position rack in bottom third of oven; preheat to 450°F. Coat a rimmed baking sheet with cooking spray.

2. Grate 2 teaspoons zest from orange. Slice 1/2 inch off the ends of the orange and squeeze the juice from them into a medium saucepan; add the zest. Set aside.

3. Cut the rest of the orange in half, then into 1/4-inch slices. Toss the orange slices in a large bowl with green beans, onion, olives, oil, wine, salt and 1/4 teaspoon pepper. Spread the mixture in an even layer on the prepared baking sheet. Toss chicken with za'atar in the bowl, then place on top of the green bean mixture.

4. Roast on the bottom rack until the green beans are tender and the chicken is no longer pink in the middle, about 15 minutes.

5. Meanwhile, add broth and the remaining 1/4 teaspoon pepper to the saucepan. Bring to a boil. Stir in couscous. Remove from heat, cover and let stand for 5 minutes. Fluff with a fork. Serve with the chicken and vegetables.

SERVES 4: 3 oz. chicken, 2 cups vegetables & 1/2 cup couscous each

Calories 436 | Fat 16g (sat 3g) | Cholesterol 63mg | Carbohydrates 43g | Total sugars 7g (added 0g) | Protein 32g | Fiber 9g | Sodium 583mg | Potassium 515mg.
Nutrition bonus: Vitamin C (56% daily value).

roast pork, asparagus & cherry tomato bowl

This Mediterranean-flavored dinner-in-a-bowl starts with lemon-scented bulgur and layers on pork and vegetables roasted side-by-side. Top it off with a drizzle of creamy hummus sauce.

2¹/₂ cups water plus 2 tablespoons, divided

1¹/₄ cups bulgur

³/₄ teaspoon salt, divided

1 pound pork tenderloin, trimmed

1 teaspoon dried marjoram

¹/₄ teaspoon ground pepper

2 tablespoons canola oil, divided

1 bunch asparagus, cut into 1-inch pieces

1 large red onion, chopped

1 cup halved cherry tomatoes

¹/₂ cup finely chopped fresh parsley

2 teaspoons lemon zest

2 tablespoons lemon juice

¹/₄ cup plain hummus (see Tip, opposite)

1. Preheat oven to 400°F.

2. Bring 2¹/₂ cups water to a boil in a medium saucepan. Remove from heat and stir in bulgur and ¹/₄ teaspoon salt. Cover and let stand until tender, about 20 minutes.

3. Meanwhile, sprinkle pork with marjoram, pepper and ¹/₄ teaspoon salt. Heat 1 tablespoon oil in a large cast-iron or other ovenproof skillet over medium-high heat. Add the pork; cook, turning often, until browned on all sides, 4 to 6 minutes.

4. Toss asparagus and onion with the remaining 1 tablespoon oil and ¹/₄ teaspoon salt in a medium bowl. When the pork is browned, scatter the asparagus and onion around it. Transfer the pan to the oven and roast until an instant-read thermometer inserted in the center of the pork registers 145°F, 12 to 16 minutes. About 5 minutes before the pork is done, scatter the tomatoes over the vegetables in the pan.

5. Transfer the pork to a clean cutting board and let rest for 5 minutes before slicing. Toss the vegetables with the pan juices.

6. Drain any remaining liquid from the bulgur, then stir in parsley, lemon zest and lemon juice. Combine hummus and 2 tablespoons hot water in a small bowl. Divide the bulgur among 4 bowls and top with the pork and vegetables; drizzle with the hummus sauce.

SERVES 4: 1 cup bulgur, 3 oz. pork, ³/₄ cup vegetables & 1¹/₂ Tbsp. sauce each

Calories 400 | Fat 12g (sat 2g) | Cholesterol 74mg | Carbohydrates 44g | Total sugars 4g (added 0g) | Protein 33g | Fiber 9g | Sodium 583mg | Potassium 985mg. Nutrition bonus: Vitamin C (44% daily value) | Folate (32% dv) | Vitamin A (30% dv) | Iron (21% dv).

shrimp & vegetable red rice salad

Bhutanese red rice has a nutty taste and pleasant chewy texture, but any type of whole-grain rice works in this hearty salad. Check the package directions: depending on the variety, red rice cooks for 20 to 50 minutes.

1 cup red rice *or* other whole-grain rice *(see Tip)*

6 tablespoons extra-virgin olive oil

4 tablespoons rice vinegar

3 tablespoons finely chopped shallot

3 tablespoons chopped fresh parsley (optional)

1½ tablespoons Dijon mustard

¾ teaspoon salt

Ground pepper to taste

2 cups cooked medium shrimp, chopped

2 cups packed coarsely chopped baby spinach

2 cups halved cherry tomatoes

1 cup thinly sliced sugar snap peas

1 cup diced radishes

½ cup crumbled feta cheese

1. Prepare rice according to package directions.

2. Meanwhile, whisk oil, vinegar, shallot, parsley (if using), mustard, salt and pepper in a large bowl.

3. When the rice is done, stir ½ cup of the vinaigrette into it, then spread it on a baking sheet and let cool to room temperature.

4. Add the cooled rice to the remaining vinaigrette along with shrimp, spinach, tomatoes, snap peas, radishes and feta; gently stir to combine.

SERVES 6: 1⅓ cups each

Calories 328 | **Fat** 17g (sat 4g) | **Cholesterol** 95mg | **Carbohydrates** 30g | **Total sugars** 3g (added 0g) | **Protein** 16g | **Fiber** 3g | **Sodium** 522mg | **Potassium** 387mg. **Nutrition bonus:** Vitamin C (36% daily value) | Vitamin A (32% dv).

clean it up

Rice contains varying levels of arsenic, a natural element found in soil and water that is associated with certain cancers and heart disease when consumed in high amounts over time. The amount of arsenic in rice varies based on the type and where it's grown, with brown rice having more than white. The bottom line? It's safe to continue eating rice, but vary your grain choices so that you're not eating rice all the time.

get together

Whether you want to catch up with friends, celebrate a birthday or entertain out-of-town guests, there's always a good reason to host a dinner party. But just because you're having company doesn't mean it has to be complicated or unhealthy. The recipes in this chapter are easy enough that you'll have plenty of time to be with your guests instead of focusing on what's on the stove. A colorful pan of baked eggs with chiles and tomatoes is perfect for vegetarians. Carne asada tacos and spicy tomato-avocado salsa let you host a taco party. And you can get people in on the assembly for spiced beef and veggie lettuce wraps. Most of the recipes in this chapter serve four people, so depending on how many people you're entertaining, scale them up accordingly.

Taco Lettuce Wraps *(page 90)*

chicken & sun-dried tomato orzo

Artichokes, sun-dried tomatoes and Pecorino Romano cheese pack a flavorful punch along with the tantalizing aroma of fresh marjoram in this rustic Italian-inspired dish.

8 ounces whole-wheat orzo

1 cup water

1/2 cup chopped sun-dried tomatoes (not packed in oil), divided

1 plum tomato, diced

1 clove garlic, peeled

3 teaspoons chopped fresh marjoram, divided

1 tablespoon red-wine vinegar

2 teaspoons extra-virgin olive oil plus 1 tablespoon, divided

4 boneless, skinless chicken breasts, trimmed (1-1 1/4 pounds)

1/4 teaspoon salt

1/4 teaspoon ground pepper

1 9-ounce package frozen artichoke hearts, thawed

1/2 cup shredded Pecorino Romano cheese, divided

1. Cook orzo in a large saucepan of boiling water until just tender, 8 to 10 minutes or according to package directions. Drain and rinse.

2. Meanwhile, place 1 cup water, 1/4 cup sun-dried tomatoes, plum tomato, garlic, 2 teaspoons marjoram, vinegar and 2 teaspoons oil in a blender. Blend until just a few chunks remain.

3. Season chicken with salt and pepper. Heat the remaining 1 tablespoon oil in a large skillet over medium-high heat. Add the chicken and cook, adjusting the heat as necessary, until golden outside and no longer pink in the middle, 3 to 5 minutes per side. Transfer to a plate; tent with foil to keep warm.

4. Pour the tomato sauce into the pan and bring to a boil. Measure out 1/2 cup sauce into a small bowl. Add the remaining 1/4 cup sun-dried tomatoes to the pan along with the orzo, artichoke hearts and 6 tablespoons cheese. Cook, stirring, until heated through, 1 to 2 minutes. Divide among 4 plates.

5. Slice the chicken. Top each portion of orzo with some sliced chicken, 2 tablespoons of the reserved tomato sauce and a sprinkling of the remaining cheese and marjoram.

SERVES 4: 3 oz. chicken & 1 cup orzo each

Calories 456 | Fat 12g (sat 3g) | Cholesterol 70mg | Carbohydrates 54g | Total sugars 4g (added 0g) | Protein 36g | Fiber 10g | Sodium 377mg | Potassium 785mg. Nutrition bonus: Folate (35% daily value) | Iron (22% dv).

To Make Ahead:
Marinate steak (Step 1) for up to 1 day. Prepare salsa (Step 2) up to 2 hours ahead.

carne asada tacos

Everyone loves a taco party, and carne asada (grilled steak) is a simple way to do it. Searing the marinated flank steak under the broiler keeps this dish quick and fuss-free, but grill it if you prefer. Cotija cheese, also called *queso añejo* or *queso añejado*, is an aged Mexican cheese similar to Parmesan. Find it near other specialty cheeses in the supermarket or in Latin grocery stores.

- 1/2 **cup white vinegar**
- 2 **tablespoons chili powder**
- 2 **tablespoons extra-virgin olive oil**
- 2³/4 **teaspoons salt, divided**
- 1 **teaspoon garlic powder**
- 2 **pounds flank** *or* **skirt steak, trimmed and cut into 3 equal portions**
- 1 **pound tomatoes, chopped**
- 2-4 **fresh jalapeño peppers** *or* **serrano chiles, seeded and finely diced**
- 1/2 **cup chopped onion**
- 1/2 **cup chopped fresh cilantro**
- 1 **slightly firm ripe avocado, diced**
- **Juice of 1 lime**
- 16 **5- to 6-inch corn** *or* **whole-wheat flour tortillas, warmed**
- 1/3 **cup crumbled Cotija cheese** *or* **other shredded cheese**

1. Whisk vinegar, chili powder, oil, 2 teaspoons salt and garlic powder in a 9-by-13-inch non-reactive baking dish (*see Tip, page 247*). Add steak and turn to coat. Cover and marinate in the refrigerator for at least 1 hour and up to 24 hours.

2. Make salsa about 20 minutes (and up to 2 hours) before cooking the steak: Gently combine tomatoes, jalapeños (or chiles) to taste, onion, cilantro, avocado, lime juice and the remaining 3/4 teaspoon salt in a medium bowl.

3. Position rack in upper third of oven; preheat broiler.

4. Place the steak on a rimmed baking sheet (discard the marinade). Broil on the upper rack 3 to 4 minutes per side for medium. Transfer to a clean cutting board and let rest for 5 minutes. Thinly slice against the grain. Serve the steak in warm tortillas and topped with the salsa and cheese.

SERVES 8: 2 tacos each

Calories 350 | Fat 14g (sat 4g) | Cholesterol 76mg | Carbohydrates 28g | Total sugars 3g (added 0g) | Protein 29g | Fiber 6g | Sodium 433mg | Potassium 773mg.
Nutrition bonus: Vitamin C (27% daily value) | Vitamin B$_{12}$ (22% dv).

seared chicken
with lemon-herb cream sauce

The creamy sauce in this recipe uses yogurt instead of cream. It pairs beautifully with pan-seared cod or salmon too. Salty-sour preserved lemons, which provide a signature flavor to many Moroccan dishes, are lemons that have been soaked in a salt-lemon mixture for at least 30 days. You can find them at specialty-food stores.

2 **teaspoons extra-virgin olive oil plus 1 tablespoon, divided**

2 **8-ounce boneless, skinless chicken breasts**

³/₄ **cup nonfat plain yogurt**

2 **tablespoons minced preserved lemon *or* 2 teaspoons lemon zest *(see Tip)***

1 **tablespoon finely chopped fresh oregano**

1 **tablespoon finely chopped fresh parsley**

¹/₄ **teaspoon salt**

¹/₄ **teaspoon ground pepper**

1. Heat 2 teaspoons oil in a medium nonstick skillet over medium heat. Add chicken and cook, turning once or twice, until browned and cooked through, 8 to 10 minutes per side.

2. Whisk the remaining 1 tablespoon oil, yogurt, preserved lemon (or zest), oregano, parsley, salt and pepper in a small bowl. Serve the chicken with the sauce.

SERVES 4: 3 oz. chicken & 2 Tbsp. sauce each

Calories 202 | Fat 9g (sat 2g) | Cholesterol 64mg | Carbohydrates 4g | Total sugars 4g (added 0g) | Protein 26g | Fiber 0g | Sodium 236mg | Potassium 320mg.

clean it up

Even though citrus isn't on the Dirty Dozen—a list provided by the Environmental Working Group (*ewg.org*) of the top 12 types of produce with the highest pesticide residues—opt for organic citrus when using the peel and zest. Pesticide residue sits on the peels of lemons and other citrus fruits. Using organic citrus minimizes the amount of pesticides that you wind up eating. No access to organic? To minimize pesticides, scrub the lemon with a vegetable brush and dry it before zesting.

fish with coconut-shallot sauce

The tropical flavors of coconut and lime are highlighted in this easy-to-prepare fish dish. Look for dried unsweetened coconut chips (also called flaked coconut) in the baking or bulk section at the supermarket or at natural-foods stores. Serve with brown rice, to soak up the sauce, and a green salad with a tangy vinaigrette.

3 large cloves garlic, chopped

3/4 teaspoon kosher salt, divided

2 tablespoons extra-virgin olive oil, divided

2 tablespoons chopped fresh thyme *or* 2 teaspoons dried

1/4 teaspoon ground pepper, plus more to taste

1 1/4 pounds mahi-mahi, red snapper *or* grouper, skinned (*see Tip, page 247*) and cut into 4 portions

2 tablespoons finely chopped shallot

1 cup "lite" coconut milk (*see Tip*)

1/4 cup unsweetened coconut chips, toasted (*see Tip, page 247*)

Lime wedges for serving

clean it up

Many brands of coconut milk contain guar gum, which helps prevent the coconut cream and water from separating. It's a source of soluble fiber derived from the seed of an Asian plant. The FDA considers gums safe, while the Center for Science in the Public Interest (CSPI) puts all gums on the "Certain People Should Avoid" list due to a lack of research. There's some evidence that they may cause bloating and other symptoms in people with digestive and bowel disorders. If you have IBS or any other digestive issues, you might want to use caution and/or minimize use of products that contain guar gum.

1. Position rack in upper third of oven; preheat broiler to high. Line a baking sheet or broiler pan with foil and coat with cooking spray.

2. Mash garlic and 1/2 teaspoon salt on a cutting board with a fork to make a paste. Combine with 1 tablespoon oil, thyme and 1/4 teaspoon pepper. Place the fish on the prepared pan and spread the paste on top of it.

3. Heat the remaining 1 tablespoon oil in a medium skillet over medium heat. Add shallot and cook, stirring, for 30 seconds. Add coconut milk, increase heat to medium-high and bring to a simmer. Reduce heat to medium-low and simmer until reduced to 3/4 cup, about 6 minutes. Season with the remaining 1/4 teaspoon salt and pepper to taste.

4. Meanwhile, broil the fish until just cooked through, 6 to 8 minutes. Spoon the sauce on top, sprinkle with coconut and serve with lime.

SERVES 4: 4 oz. fish & 3 Tbsp. sauce each

Calories 270 | Fat 15g (sat 7g) | Cholesterol 103mg | Carbohydrates 7g | Total sugars 1g (added 0g) | Protein 28g | Fiber 1g | Sodium 351mg | Potassium 643mg.

broiled ginger-lime chicken

ACTIVE | 20 min
TOTAL | 2 hrs 40 min
(including 2 hrs marinating time)

To Make Ahead:
Marinate chicken
(Step 2) for up to 1 day.

A flavorful paste of cinnamon, nutmeg, ginger and lime makes this chicken taste like it's straight out of the Caribbean. Serve with rice pilaf *(page 162)* and a side of seasoned black beans.

6 large *or* **12 small bone-in chicken thighs (2^1/$_2$-3 pounds), skin removed**

^{1}/$_4$ cup finely chopped scallions

2 tablespoons finely chopped fresh ginger

2 tablespoons canola oil

1 tablespoon lime zest

2 tablespoons lime juice

1 teaspoon ground cinnamon

1 teaspoon salt

^{1}/$_2$ teaspoon ground pepper

^{1}/$_2$ teaspoon ground nutmeg

^{1}/$_8$ teaspoon cayenne pepper

1. Line a broiler pan or rimmed baking sheet with foil and coat with cooking spray.

2. Pat chicken dry. Place on the prepared pan, skinned-side up. Mix scallions, ginger, oil, lime zest and juice, cinnamon, salt, pepper, nutmeg and cayenne in a small bowl and spread on the chicken. Cover and refrigerate for 2 to 24 hours.

3. Preheat broiler to high.

4. Broil the chicken on the pan until an instant-read thermometer inserted in the thickest part registers 165°F, 15 to 25 minutes.

SERVES 6: 1 large or 2 small thighs each

Calories 218 | Fat 13g (sat 3g) | Cholesterol 77mg | Carbohydrates 3g | Total sugars 0g (added 0g) | Protein 22g | Fiber 1g | Sodium 453mg | Potassium 200mg.

quick lentil salmon salad

Seared salmon on a bed of vinegary lentils is a classic French bistro dish. This budget-friendly version combines flaked canned salmon and buttery brown lentils seasoned with garlicky vinaigrette. Because this dish uses ingredients you likely have on hand, it makes a great choice for a dinner party on the fly.

³/₄ cup brown lentils

¹/₂ cup chopped red onion plus ¹/₄ cup thinly sliced, divided

2 cloves garlic, minced

³/₄ teaspoon salt

¹/₄ cup extra-virgin olive oil

3 tablespoons red-wine vinegar

³/₄ teaspoon dried thyme

¹/₄ teaspoon ground pepper

1 15-ounce can wild salmon, drained

1 cup carrot ribbons

1 cup sliced celery

4 lemon wedges for serving

1. Bring a medium saucepan of water to a boil. Add lentils and chopped onion, reduce heat to maintain a lively simmer and cook until the lentils are just tender, 11 to 13 minutes. Drain well.

2. Meanwhile, mash garlic and salt into a paste with the side of a chef's knife (or a fork). Transfer to a medium bowl and whisk in oil, vinegar, thyme and pepper.

3. Remove any skin and/or bones from salmon; flake the salmon into a large bowl. Add sliced onion, carrot and 3 tablespoons of the dressing; gently toss to coat. Add celery and the lentils to the remaining dressing; gently stir to combine. Divide the lentils among 4 bowls, top with the salmon salad and serve with lemon wedges.

SERVES 4: 1¹/₂ cups each

Calories 341 | Fat 15g (sat 2g) | Cholesterol 24mg | Carbohydrates 25g | Total sugars 4g (added 0g) | Protein 26g | Fiber 9g | Sodium 723mg | Potassium 529mg. Nutrition bonus: Folate (52% daily value) | Vitamin A (44% dv) | Iron (29% dv).

roasted halibut
with tangerine & olive tapenade

Sweet tangerines balance briny olive tapenade, making a flavor-packed topping for meaty white fish. The tapenade is also terrific on roasted chicken or grilled lamb.

3-5 **Pixie tangerines** *or* **clementines, divided**

¼ cup pitted Kalamata *or* green olives

1 teaspoon capers, rinsed

1 small clove garlic, minced

1 teaspoon finely chopped fresh thyme

1 tablespoon extra-virgin olive oil

1¼ pounds halibut *(see Tip, below)*, **skinned** *(see Tip, page 247)* **and cut into 4 portions**

½ teaspoon kosher salt

½ teaspoon ground pepper

 clean it up

Atlantic halibut has been overfished and isn't available commercially. For a sustainable choice, opt for Pacific halibut with the blue Marine Stewardship Council certification seal. Large cold-water fish like halibut are higher in methylmercury, a heavy metal that can damage the brain, heart, kidney, liver and nervous system if consumed in excess *(see Buyer's Guide, page 252)*.

1. Preheat oven to 400°F. Line a rimmed baking sheet with parchment paper.

2. Grate ½ teaspoon zest from 1 tangerine (or clementine) and squeeze 1 tablespoon juice. Coarsely chop olives, capers, garlic, thyme and the zest together on a cutting board (or process in a mini food processor). Transfer to a small bowl; stir in oil and the citrus juice.

3. Peel the remaining fruit and cut into ¼-inch slices. Arrange 4 "beds" of slices on the prepared pan, making them about the size of each portion of fish. Place a piece of fish, skinned-side down, on each bed. Sprinkle the fish with salt and pepper, then spread about 1 tablespoon of the tapenade on each portion.

4. Bake the fish until the thickest part flakes with a fork, 8 to 10 minutes per inch of thickness.

SERVES 4: 4 oz. fish each

Calories 211 | Fat 7g (sat 1g) | Cholesterol 69mg | Carbohydrates 8g | Total sugars 5g (added 0g) | Protein 27g | Fiber 1g | Sodium 360mg | Potassium 731mg. Nutrition bonus: Vitamin C (49% daily value) | Vitamin B$_{12}$ (26% dv).

baked eggs, tomatoes & chiles {shakshuka}

This popular Israeli breakfast or brunch dish features eggs cooked on a bed of roasted tomato sauce. It's also great for a casual vegetarian dinner get-together. Serve with warm crusty bread.

3 cloves garlic, divided

3 pounds ripe plum tomatoes, cut into ¹/₂-inch pieces

1 medium onion, finely chopped

4 tablespoons extra-virgin olive oil, divided

2 tablespoons chopped fresh parsley, plus more for garnish

³/₄ teaspoon salt, divided

¹/₂ teaspoon ground pepper, divided

2 large green chiles, such as Anaheim, finely chopped

1 teaspoon ground cumin

¹/₃ cup chopped fresh basil

4 large eggs

¹/₂ cup crumbled feta cheese

Hot sauce for serving

1. Preheat oven to 450°F.

2. Slice 2 garlic cloves and toss with tomatoes, onion, 3 tablespoons oil, parsley and ¹/₄ teaspoon each salt and pepper in a large bowl. Spread evenly on a large rimmed baking sheet or in a shallow roasting pan. Roast until the tomatoes are shriveled and browned, about 45 minutes.

3. Chop the remaining garlic clove. Heat the remaining 1 tablespoon oil in a large skillet over medium heat. Add the garlic and chiles; cook, stirring, for 2 minutes. Add cumin and cook, stirring, for 30 seconds. Stir in the tomato mixture, the remaining ¹/₂ teaspoon salt and basil. Bring to a simmer and cook, stirring occasionally, until the tomatoes are mostly broken down, 6 to 8 minutes.

4. Make 4 deep indentations in the sauce with the back of a spoon and carefully crack an egg into each. Sprinkle the eggs with the remaining ¹/₄ teaspoon pepper. Cover and cook over medium-low until the whites are set, 6 to 8 minutes.

5. Remove from heat, sprinkle with feta and let stand, covered, for 2 minutes. (The eggs will continue to cook a bit as they stand.) Garnish with parsley and serve with hot sauce, if desired.

SERVES 4: 1 egg & 1 cup sauce each

Calories 330 | Fat 24g (sat 6g) | Cholesterol 203mg | Carbohydrates 19g | Total sugars 11g (added 0g) | Protein 13g | Fiber 5g | Sodium 700mg | Potassium 965mg. Nutrition bonus: Vitamin C (171% daily value) | Vitamin A (71% dv) | Folate (23% dv).

sweet potato carbonara
with spinach & mushrooms

ACTIVE 40 minutes
TOTAL 40 minutes

To Make Ahead:
Refrigerate the raw "noodles"
(Step 2) for up to 1 day.

Equipment:
Spiral vegetable slicer or
julienne vegetable peeler

In this veggie-driven take on carbonara, "spiralized" sweet potato noodles replace traditional pasta. Spinach is called for here, but any dark leafy green, such as kale, chard or collards, would also be a nice addition.

2 pounds sweet potatoes, peeled

3 large eggs, beaten

1 cup grated Parmesan cheese

1/4 teaspoon salt

1/4 teaspoon ground pepper, plus more for serving

1 tablespoon extra-virgin olive oil

3 thin slices prosciutto, chopped

1 8-ounce package sliced mushrooms

2 cloves garlic, minced

1 5-ounce package baby spinach

1. Put a large pot of water on to boil.

2. Using a spiral vegetable slicer or julienne vegetable peeler, cut sweet potatoes lengthwise into long, thin strands. You should have about 12 cups of "noodles."

3. Cook the sweet potatoes in the boiling water, gently stirring once or twice, until just starting to soften but not completely tender, 1 1/2 to 3 minutes. Reserve 1/4 cup of the cooking water, then drain. Return the noodles to the pot, off the heat. Combine eggs, Parmesan, salt, pepper and the reserved water in a bowl; pour over the noodles and gently toss with tongs until evenly coated.

4. Heat oil in a large skillet over medium heat. Add prosciutto and mushrooms and cook, stirring often, until the liquid has evaporated and the mushrooms are starting to brown, 6 to 8 minutes. Add garlic and cook, stirring, until fragrant, about 1 minute. Add spinach and cook, stirring, until wilted, 1 to 2 minutes. Add the vegetables to the noodles and toss to combine. Top with a generous grinding of pepper.

SERVES 5: 1 2/3 cups each

Calories 310 | **Fat** 12g (sat 4g) | **Cholesterol** 132mg | **Carbohydrates** 38g | **Total sugars** 12g (added 0g) | **Protein** 16g | **Fiber** 6g | **Sodium** 749mg | **Potassium** 796mg. **Nutrition bonus:** Vitamin A (631% daily value) | Vitamin C (55% dv) | Calcium (23% dv) | Folate (22% dv).

taco lettuce wraps

These do-it-yourself lettuce wraps are fun food for a group. Set out bowls of the seasoned meat, lettuce leaves, salsa and veggies, and invite your guests to create their own tacos. Add other veggies to the mix, like corn kernels, shredded carrots or sliced jalapeños. (*Photo: page 70.*)

- **8** small Boston lettuce leaves *or* **4** large, cut in half crosswise
- **1** tablespoon canola oil
- **1** pound lean ground beef
- **1/4** teaspoon salt
- **5** tablespoons prepared salsa (*see Tip*)
- **1** tablespoon rice vinegar
- **1 1/2** teaspoons ground cumin
- **1** cup diced avocado
- **1** cup julienned jicama
- **1/4** cup finely diced red onion

1. Wash and dry lettuce well.

2. Heat oil in a large nonstick skillet over medium-high heat. Add ground beef, season with salt and cook, stirring often, until cooked through, 4 to 6 minutes.

3. Meanwhile, whisk salsa, vinegar and cumin in a small bowl.

4. Remove the pan from the heat, add the salsa mixture and stir to combine. Serve in the lettuce leaves, topped with avocado, jicama and onion.

SERVES 4: 2 wraps each

Calories 291 | **Fat** 19g (sat 5g) | **Cholesterol** 72mg | **Carbohydrates** 8g | **Total sugars** 2g (added 0g) | **Protein** 23g | **Fiber** 4g | **Sodium** 348mg | **Potassium** 579mg. **Nutrition bonus**: Vitamin B$_{12}$ (35% daily value).

clean it up

Store-bought salsa can be a surprising source of added sugar and high amounts of sodium. Look for a brand that contains no added sweeteners and has less than 150 mg of sodium per 2-tablespoon serving. Some brands use calcium chloride as a preservative (it keeps the tomatoes from getting mushy). This calcium salt, a common electrolyte, is safe and even contributes some calcium to the products it's in.

indian edamame quinoa burgers

ACTIVE | 35 min
TOTAL | 35 min

To Make Ahead:
Individually wrap and freeze cooked burgers for up to 3 months. Unwrap and bake frozen burgers on an oiled baking sheet at 375°F for 20 minutes, turning once.

Topped with a quick cucumber and yogurt raita, these meatless patties are a great alternative to traditional burgers. Experiment with different seasonings in place of the ginger and garam masala—garlic and cumin for Middle Eastern flair or garlic and chili powder for a Southwestern spin. Serve with a big spinach salad.

- 1/2 cup quinoa
- 1 cup water
- 8 ounces frozen edamame (about 1 1/2 cups), thawed
- 3 scallions, chopped, divided
- 1 large egg
- 1 tablespoon minced fresh ginger
- 1 1/4 teaspoons garam masala
- 1/2 teaspoon salt plus 1/8 teaspoon, divided
- 1/4 teaspoon cayenne pepper
- 2 tablespoons extra-virgin olive oil, divided
- 3/4 cup low-fat plain yogurt
- 1/2 cup chopped English cucumber
- 1/4 cup chopped fresh cilantro (optional)
- 1/4 teaspoon ground pepper
- 1 very large tomato, cut into 4 thick slices

1. Combine quinoa and water in a small saucepan. Bring to a boil. Reduce heat, cover and simmer until the water has been absorbed, about 15 minutes. Remove from heat and let stand 5 minutes.

2. Transfer the quinoa to a food processor; add edamame, 2 chopped scallions, egg, ginger, garam masala, 1/2 teaspoon salt and cayenne. Pulse until well combined. Form into four 3 1/2-inch patties (a generous 1/2 cup each).

3. Heat 1 tablespoon oil in a large nonstick skillet over medium-high heat; swirl to coat the pan. Reduce heat to medium and add the burgers. Cook until browned on one side, 3 to 4 minutes. Carefully turn them over, swirl in the remaining 1 tablespoon oil and cook until brown on the other side, 3 to 4 minutes more.

4. Meanwhile, combine yogurt, cucumber, cilantro (if using), pepper and the remaining scallion and 1/8 teaspoon salt in a bowl. Serve each burger on a tomato slice with the yogurt sauce.

SERVES 4: 1 burger, 1 tomato slice & 1/4 cup sauce each

Calories 285 | Fat 13g (sat 2g) | Cholesterol 49mg | Carbohydrates 29g | Total sugars 9g (added 0g) | Protein 15g | Fiber 6g | Sodium 427mg | Potassium 822mg. Nutrition bonus: Folate (63% daily value) | Vitamin C (37% dv) | Vitamin A (29% dv).

cleaned-up classics

We all crave comfort foods at times, but they don't typically rank high on health marks. Many are loaded with sodium, added sugars or sketchy processed ingredients. (Just check the nutrition info on that fast-food taco salad if you need proof.) When you make your favorite comfort dishes at home, though, you control what goes into them. Over the years we've perfected making classics with nutritious, whole ingredients so you can enjoy the comfort foods you love and still eat clean. Our bag of tricks includes loading up on vegetables, herbs and spices, and limiting sugar and salt without losing any flavor.

For instance, in this chapter you'll find mac and cheese that's blended with sweet potato for natural sweetness and to give it that special orange hue. Baked potatoes and potpies are updated with plenty of nutrient-rich greens. You can even make your own "corned" beef—with no preservatives and significantly less sodium, but with all the savory richness.

Pork Chops with Creamy Mushroom Sauce (*page 99*)

ACTIVE 30 min
TOTAL 30 min

To Make Ahead: Refrigerate for up to 3 days or freeze for up to 3 months.

spaghetti
with quick meat sauce

Instead of opening a jar of sauce, try this low-effort meat sauce on a weeknight. Serve it over whole-wheat spaghetti with steamed broccoli and garlic bread for a classic meal. The recipe makes enough for 8 servings, so if you're serving only four for dinner, cook 8 ounces of spaghetti and freeze the leftover sauce.

1 **pound whole-wheat spaghetti**

2 **teaspoons extra-virgin olive oil**

1 **large onion, finely chopped**

1 **large carrot, finely chopped**

1 **stalk celery, finely chopped**

4 **cloves garlic, minced**

1 **tablespoon Italian seasoning**

1 **pound lean (90% *or* leaner) ground beef**

1 **28-ounce can crushed tomatoes**

1/4 **cup chopped flat-leaf parsley**

1/2 **teaspoon salt**

1/2 **cup grated Parmesan cheese**

   Fresh basil for garnish

1. Bring a large pot of water to a boil. Cook pasta until just tender, 8 to 10 minutes or according to package directions. Drain.

2. Meanwhile, heat oil in a large skillet over medium heat. Add onion, carrot and celery and cook, stirring occasionally, until the onion is beginning to brown, 5 to 8 minutes.

3. Stir in garlic and Italian seasoning; cook until fragrant, about 30 seconds. Add beef and cook, stirring and breaking up with a spoon, until no longer pink, 3 to 5 minutes. Increase heat to high. Stir in tomatoes and cook until thickened, 4 to 6 minutes. Stir in parsley and salt.

4. Serve the sauce over the pasta, sprinkled with cheese. Garnish with basil, if desired.

SERVES 8: 1 cup pasta & generous 3/4 cup sauce each

Calories 365 | Fat 9g (sat 3g) | Cholesterol 40mg | Carbohydrates 54g | Total sugars 8g (added 0g) | Protein 23g | Fiber 10g | Sodium 426mg | Potassium 655mg. Nutrition bonus: Vitamin A (39% daily value) | Iron (27% dv) | Vitamin C (24% dv).

ACTIVE 45 min
TOTAL 1 hr 20 min

To Make Ahead: Prepare
through Step 2; refrigerate for
up to 1 day. Let stand at room
temperature for 30 minutes
before finishing.

kale & white bean
potpie with chive biscuits

In this vegetarian potpie, homemade chive biscuits top a savory mixture of hearty white beans
and kale. If you like, add a little shredded Gruyère or Cheddar cheese to the biscuit dough. The
biscuits are also great on their own.

FILLING

- **2 tablespoons extra-virgin olive oil**
- **1 cup chopped onion**
- **¹/₂ cup chopped carrot**
- **¹/₂ cup chopped celery**
- **3 cloves garlic, minced**
- **2 teaspoons chopped fresh thyme** *or*
  ³/₄ teaspoon dried
- **1 teaspoon chopped fresh rosemary** *or*
  ¹/₄ teaspoon dried
- **8 cups chopped kale (1 small-to-medium bunch)**
- **¹/₄ cup white whole-wheat flour**
- **3 cups low-sodium vegetable broth** *or*
  no-chicken broth
- **1 15-ounce can white beans, rinsed**
- **¹/₂ teaspoon kosher salt**
- **¹/₂ teaspoon ground pepper**

BISCUITS

- **1 cup white whole-wheat flour**
- **1 teaspoon baking powder**
- **¹/₄ teaspoon baking soda**
- **¹/₄ teaspoon kosher salt**
- **¹/₄ teaspoon ground pepper**
- **3 tablespoons cold unsalted butter,
  cut into small pieces**
- **3 tablespoons minced fresh chives**
- **¹/₂ cup cold buttermilk**
- **2 teaspoons extra-virgin olive oil**

1. To prepare filling: Preheat oven to 350°F. Coat
   a 10-inch cast-iron skillet (or similar-size 2-quart
   baking dish) with cooking spray.

2. Heat 2 tablespoons oil in a large pot over
   medium heat. Add onion, carrot and celery and
   cook, stirring occasionally, until the vegetables
   are soft, 4 to 6 minutes. Add garlic, thyme and
   rosemary; cook, stirring, until fragrant, about
   30 seconds. Add kale; cook, stirring often, until

continued

tender and wilted, 3 to 5 minutes. Sprinkle with ¼ cup flour and cook, stirring, for 30 seconds. Stir in broth, increase heat to high and bring to a boil. Reduce heat and simmer, stirring, until thickened, about 2 minutes. Stir in beans and ½ teaspoon each salt and pepper. Transfer the mixture to the prepared pan.

3. **To prepare biscuits:** Whisk flour, baking powder, baking soda, salt and pepper in a large bowl. Using a pastry blender or your fingertips, cut or rub butter into the dry ingredients. Stir in chives. Add buttermilk and stir until just combined. Form the dough into 6 biscuits and place on top of the filling. Lightly brush with oil.

4. Place the potpie on a baking sheet. Bake until the biscuits are lightly browned and the filling is bubbling, about 30 minutes. Let cool 5 minutes before serving.

SERVES 6: about 1¼ cups filling & 1 biscuit each

Calories 277 | **Fat** 13g (sat 5g) | **Cholesterol** 16mg | **Carbohydrates** 37g | **Total sugars** 5g (added 0g) | **Protein** 9g | **Fiber** 8g | **Sodium** 550mg | **Potassium** 457mg. **Nutrition bonus:** Vitamin A (84% daily value) | Vitamin C (51% dv) | Iron (27% dv) | Folate (23% dv).

 clean it up

Some cuts of pork, such as the tenderloin and boneless loin, may be treated with a sodium-and-water solution to improve flavor, texture and color, as well as extend shelf life. Pork chops don't typically receive this treatment, but ask your butcher to be sure. If they're packaged, check the ingredients. The solution must be disclosed on the label and will provide a percent of the solution and its ingredients, such as sodium phosphate, vinegar and salt. It's a safe addition according to the USDA and FDA, but does add more sodium to your dish, so you may not want to salt the meat as much.

pork chops
with creamy mushroom sauce

For this entree, pan-seared bone-in pork chops are topped with a rich and creamy mushroom sauce flavored with fresh herbs. (No canned condensed soup here!) The pork chops cook quickly over high heat, so choose a heavy pan, such as cast-iron, to achieve a nice crusty exterior without overcooking the meat. *(Photo: page 92.)*

4 bone-in pork chops, $^1/_2$-$^3/_4$ inch thick (about 2 pounds), trimmed *(see Tip, opposite)*

$^1/_2$ teaspoon salt, divided

$^1/_2$ teaspoon ground pepper

3 tablespoons extra-virgin olive oil, divided

$^1/_3$ cup minced shallots

8 ounces sliced mixed mushrooms, such as cremini, shiitake and oyster

$^1/_2$ cup dry white wine

$^1/_3$ cup half-and-half

$^1/_2$ cup chopped fresh herbs, such as chives, tarragon *and/or* parsley

1. Sprinkle pork chops with $^1/_4$ teaspoon salt and pepper. Heat 1 tablespoon oil in a large cast-iron skillet over medium-high heat. Reduce heat to medium and add 2 pork chops. Cook, turning once, until cooked through, 5 to 7 minutes total. Transfer to a plate and tent with foil. Repeat with another 1 tablespoon oil and the remaining chops.

2. Add the remaining 1 tablespoon oil to the pan. Add shallots and mushrooms; cook, stirring frequently, until the mushrooms are browned, 2 to 4 minutes. Add wine and the remaining $^1/_4$ teaspoon salt; cook, scraping up any browned bits, until the liquid has mostly evaporated, 1 to 3 minutes. Stir in half-and-half and herbs; cook until bubbling, about 1 minute more. Serve the chops with the mushroom sauce.

SERVES 4: 1 pork chop & about $^1/_3$ cup sauce each

Calories 357 | **Fat** 21g (sat 6g) | **Cholesterol** 74mg | **Carbohydrates** 6g | **Total sugars** 3g (added 0g) | **Protein** 29g | **Fiber** 1g | **Sodium** 362mg | **Potassium** 639mg.

8-layer taco salad

We updated this favorite with ground turkey in place of beef, Greek yogurt instead of sour cream and way more vegetables than is typical. Serve in a clear glass bowl to show off the layers for an eye-catching potluck dish.

1 tablespoon canola oil

1 pound 93%-lean ground turkey

2 tablespoons chili powder

1/2 teaspoon salt, divided

1 ripe avocado

1/2 cup nonfat plain Greek yogurt

1 1/2 cups crumbled unsalted tortilla chips

1 cup prepared salsa

1 15-ounce can pinto beans, rinsed

5 cups thinly sliced romaine lettuce

1/2 cup shredded Mexican cheese blend (*see Tip*)

1 medium tomato, chopped

1. Heat oil in a large skillet over medium-high heat. Add turkey, chili powder and 1/4 teaspoon salt. Cook, stirring and breaking up lumps, until cooked through, about 5 minutes.

2. Meanwhile, mash avocado, yogurt and the remaining 1/4 teaspoon salt in a small bowl with a fork until smooth.

3. Transfer the turkey and pan juices to a serving bowl. Layer chips, salsa, beans and lettuce over the turkey. Spread the avocado mixture over the lettuce. Top with cheese, then tomato.

SERVES 6: about 1 2/3 cups each

Calories 397 | **Fat** 22g (sat 5g) | **Cholesterol** 66mg | **Carbohydrates** 29g | **Total sugars** 2g (added 0g) | **Protein** 24g | **Fiber** 8g | **Sodium** 664mg | **Potassium** 822mg. **Nutrition bonus:** Vitamin A (96% daily value) | Folate (34% dv) | Iron (22% dv) | Vitamin B$_{12}$ (20% dv).

 *clean it up*

You'll notice anti-caking ingredients (usually powdered cellulose) and mold inhibitors (usually natamycin) in the ingredient lists of some preshredded cheeses. These ingredients are considered safe by the FDA and the Center for Science in the Public Interest (CSPI). However, if you want to avoid them, shred cheese at home.

clean it up

Cooking sprays contain propellants, which are hydro-carbons like butane and propane, and small quantities do make it into your food, but in amounts the FDA deems safe. These same propellants can also contribute, albeit minimally, to ground-level ozone (the main component of smog). To skip propellants, opt instead for a pump-spray bottle you fill with your own oil.

oven-fried beef taquitos

By baking taquitos in a hot oven, we found a way to still achieve that crispy, crave-worthy shell. A seasoned beef and zucchini filling and sharp Cheddar give this dish loads of flavor. Don't worry if some of the taquitos crack open while baking—they'll still be delicious. Serve with your favorite salsa, guacamole and sour cream.

1 **medium zucchini**

2 **teaspoons canola oil**

1 **pound extra-lean ground beef**

3 **tablespoons chili powder**

1 **tablespoon onion powder**

1 **teaspoon ground cumin**

1/2 **teaspoon salt**

12 **6-inch corn tortillas**

Canola oil cooking spray (*see Tip, opposite*)

3/4 **cup shredded sharp Cheddar cheese**

1. Preheat oven to 425°F.

2. Shred zucchini using the large holes of a box grater. Squeeze dry in a clean kitchen towel (you should have about 2 cups). Heat oil in a large nonstick skillet over medium-high heat. Add the zucchini, beef, chili powder, onion powder, cumin and salt. Cook, stirring, until the beef is cooked through, 5 to 7 minutes.

3. Spread tortillas out on a baking sheet in 2 overlapping rows. Bake until hot, about 2 minutes. Transfer to a plate and cover.

4. Coat the baking sheet with cooking spray. Place 6 tortillas on a clean cutting board. Working quickly, spread a generous 1/4 cup beef mixture along the bottom third of a tortilla, sprinkle with about 1 tablespoon cheese and tightly roll into a cigar shape. Place the taquito seam-side down on the baking sheet. Repeat with the remaining tortillas, filling and cheese. Generously coat the tops and sides of the taquitos with cooking spray.

5. Bake the taquitos until browned and crispy, 14 to 18 minutes.

SERVES 4: 3 taquitos each

Calories 500 | **Fat** 24g (sat 8g) | **Cholesterol** 92mg | **Carbohydrates** 40g | **Total sugars** 2g (added 0g) | **Protein** 33g | **Fiber** 7g | **Sodium** 691mg | **Potassium** 662mg. **Nutrition bonus:** Vitamin A (42% daily value) | Vitamin B$_{12}$ (37% dv) | Iron (27% dv) | Calcium (24% dv).

sweet potato macaroni & cheese

Nutrient-rich sweet potato is used as the foundation for the cheese sauce in this recipe. The bright orange color tricks your eyes into thinking it's loaded with cheese, but there's actually only about half as much cheese as there is in a traditional recipe.

 8 ounces whole-wheat elbow noodles (2 cups)
 1 medium sweet potato (about 12 ounces)
 2 cups nonfat milk
 2 tablespoons white whole-wheat flour
 1 small clove garlic, minced
1¼ cups shredded sharp Cheddar cheese
 1 tablespoon Dijon mustard
 ¼ teaspoon salt
 ¼ teaspoon ground pepper
 ½ cup frozen peas, thawed
 3 tablespoons coarse dry whole-wheat breadcrumbs (see Tip, opposite)
 1 teaspoon extra-virgin olive oil

1. Position a rack in upper third of oven; preheat broiler. Coat a 2-quart broiler-safe baking dish with cooking spray.

2. Bring a large saucepan of water to a boil. Cook pasta until just tender, 7 to 9 minutes. Drain and set aside.

3. Meanwhile, prick sweet potato with a fork in several places. Microwave on High until tender all the way to the center, 7 to 10 minutes.

4. Whisk milk, flour and garlic in a large saucepan. Heat over medium heat, whisking frequently, until steaming and hot, but not boiling. Remove from heat.

5. As soon as the sweet potato is cool enough to handle, cut open and scoop the flesh into the steaming milk. Puree with an immersion blender until smooth. (Alternatively, transfer to a blender and puree just until smooth, then return to the pot; use caution when pureeing hot liquids.)

6. Add cheese, mustard, salt and pepper and stir until the cheese has melted. Add the pasta and peas to the sauce and stir to coat. Transfer to the prepared baking dish. Combine breadcrumbs and oil and sprinkle over the pasta. Broil until the top is lightly browned and crispy, 1 to 2 minutes.

SERVES 4: about 1¼ cups each

Calories 486 | Fat 14g (sat 7g) | Cholesterol 38mg | Carbohydrates 68g | Total sugars 13g (added 0g) | Protein 24g | Fiber 10g | Sodium 549mg | Potassium 641mg. Nutrition bonus: Vitamin A (218% daily value) | Calcium (45% dv) | Vitamin C (22% dv).

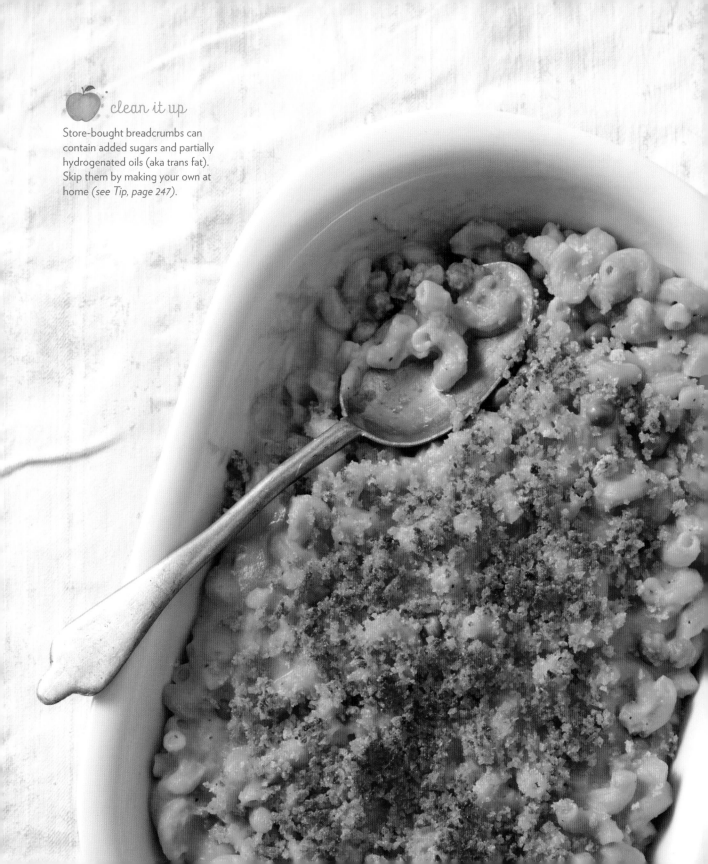

clean it up

Store-bought breadcrumbs can contain added sugars and partially hydrogenated oils (aka trans fat). Skip them by making your own at home (see Tip, page 247).

quick fettuccine alfredo

We lighten Alfredo sauce by using yogurt instead of cream. If you like, use any whole-wheat pasta shape in place of the fettuccine.

8 **ounces whole-wheat fettuccine**

1 **tablespoon butter**

1 **clove garlic, minced**

3/4 **cup nonfat plain Greek yogurt**

3/4 **cup shredded Parmesan cheese, divided**

1 **tablespoon chopped fresh parsley**

1/4 **teaspoon salt**

1/4 **teaspoon ground pepper**

1/8 **teaspoon ground nutmeg**

1. Bring a large saucepan of water to a boil. Cook pasta according to package directions. Reserve 1/2 cup of the cooking water, then drain the pasta.

2. Melt butter in a large saucepan over medium heat. Add garlic and cook for 1 minute. Stir in the reserved water and remove from heat. Whisk in yogurt, 1/2 cup cheese, parsley, salt, pepper and nutmeg. Add the pasta and toss well. Serve topped with the remaining 1/4 cup cheese.

SERVES 4: 1 cup each

Calories 312 | Fat 8g (sat 5g) | Cholesterol 21mg | Carbohydrates 45g | Total sugars 4g (added 0g) | Protein 18g | Fiber 7g | Sodium 421mg | Potassium 207mg. Nutrition bonus: Calcium (26% daily value).

crispy chicken schnitzel
with herb-brown butter

Schnitzel—a crispy breaded chicken, veal or pork cutlet—gets its name from German-speaking countries, but is found in cuisines worldwide. Our chicken schnitzel is coated with fresh whole-wheat breadcrumbs and oven "fried" using a mist of olive oil cooking spray. Serve on a bed of mixed greens or with mashed potatoes.

Olive oil cooking spray

2 8-ounce boneless, skinless chicken breasts, trimmed

1/2 teaspoon salt, divided

1/2 teaspoon ground pepper, divided

1/4 cup white whole-wheat flour

2 large eggs, beaten

1 lemon

2 cups fresh whole-wheat breadcrumbs (*see Tip, page 247*)

2 tablespoons unsalted butter

1 tablespoon extra-virgin olive oil

1 small shallot, minced

1/4 cup chopped fresh herbs, such as dill, parsley *and/or* chives

1. Preheat oven to 450°F. Coat a large baking sheet with cooking spray.

2. Cut chicken breasts in half horizontally. Cover with a large piece of plastic wrap and pound with the smooth side of a meat mallet or a heavy saucepan to an even 1/4-inch thickness. Sprinkle the chicken with 1/4 teaspoon each salt and pepper.

3. Place flour in one shallow dish and eggs in another. Zest lemon and combine the zest with breadcrumbs in a third shallow dish. (Slice the lemon for serving; set aside.) Coat both sides of the chicken in the flour, shaking off any excess, then dip in egg. Coat on both sides with the breadcrumbs, pressing to help them stick. Place the chicken on the prepared baking sheet. Coat on both sides with cooking spray.

4. Bake the chicken until golden brown and no longer pink in the center, 10 to 12 minutes.

5. Meanwhile, melt butter in a small saucepan over medium-high heat. Cook until just beginning to brown, about 2 minutes. Add oil and shallot; cook for 30 seconds more. Remove from heat; add herbs and the remaining 1/4 teaspoon each salt and pepper. Serve the chicken with the herb sauce and lemon slices.

SERVES 4: 1 cutlet & 1 Tbsp. sauce each

Calories 315 | Fat 14g (sat 5g) | Cholesterol 140mg | Carbohydrates 16g | Total sugars 0g (added 0g) | Protein 28g | Fiber 1g | Sodium 489mg | Potassium 254mg.

spanakopita loaded potatoes

This veggie-forward take on twice-baked potatoes calls for plenty of vitamin-rich spinach, plus a tasty dose of garlic and oregano. Feta and just a touch of cream cheese provide richness while still keeping this dish lean.

4 **medium russet potatoes (8-10 ounces each), scrubbed**

1 **tablespoon extra-virgin olive oil**

1 **cup diced onion**

1 **pound fresh spinach, finely chopped, *or* 4 cups frozen chopped spinach (thawed)**

3 **cloves garlic, minced**

1 **tablespoon chopped fresh oregano *or* 1 teaspoon dried**

¹/₃ **cup cream cheese**

³/₄ **teaspoon ground pepper**

¹/₄ **teaspoon kosher salt**

1 **cup crumbled feta cheese, divided**

1. Preheat oven to 400°F.

2. Pierce potatoes in several places with a fork. Bake directly on the center rack until tender, 50 to 60 minutes. Let stand until cool enough to handle.

3. Meanwhile, heat oil in a large pot over medium heat. Add onion and cook, stirring occasionally, until soft, 2 to 4 minutes. Add spinach, garlic and oregano; cook, stirring, until hot, about 4 minutes. Remove from heat.

4. Reduce oven temperature to 375°F.

5. Cut the potatoes in half lengthwise and scoop the insides into a bowl. Place the skins in a 9-by-13-inch baking pan. Add cream cheese, pepper and salt to the bowl. Beat with a hand mixer or mash with a potato masher until smooth. Stir in the spinach mixture and ¹/₂ cup feta. Stuff each potato skin with about ³/₄ cup of the filling. Top each with 1 tablespoon of the remaining feta.

6. Bake until the filling is steaming and the feta is browned, 25 to 35 minutes.

SERVES 4: 2 stuffed halves each

Calories 412 | **Fat** 19g (sat 10g) | **Cholesterol** 55mg | **Carbohydrates** 48g | **Total sugars** 6g (added 0g) | **Protein** 15g | **Fiber** 7g | **Sodium** 600mg | **Potassium** 1,712mg. **Nutrition bonus:** Vitamin A (222% daily value) | Vitamin C (84% dv) | Folate (72% dv) | Calcium (37% dv) | Iron (30% dv).

quick "corned" beef & cabbage

Traditional corned beef and cabbage sure is tasty, but it's typically loaded with preservatives and sodium. In this makeover, we slash more than a day's worth of sodium by skipping store-bought corned beef and instead starting with fresh skirt steak that we doctor with ground pickling spice. You get the flavors of corned beef without the additives or all that sodium.

2 tablespoons pickling spice

1 teaspoon dry mustard

1 teaspoon kosher salt

1/2 teaspoon ground pepper, divided

1/2 small cabbage, cored and cut into wedges

8 small carrots, trimmed

2 cups halved baby potatoes

4 tablespoons extra-virgin olive oil, divided

2 tablespoons malt vinegar *or* white-wine vinegar

1 tablespoon chopped fresh dill, plus more for garnish

1 teaspoon whole-grain mustard

1 pound skirt steak, trimmed

1. Preheat oven to 450°F.

2. Grind pickling spice in a clean spice grinder (or coffee grinder); transfer to a small bowl and combine with dry mustard, salt and 1/4 teaspoon pepper. Toss cabbage, carrots and potatoes in a large bowl with half the spice mixture and 2 tablespoons oil. Transfer to a large rimmed baking sheet. Roast, stirring once, until tender, 25 to 30 minutes.

3. Meanwhile, whisk 1 tablespoon oil, vinegar, dill, mustard and the remaining 1/4 teaspoon pepper in a small bowl to make a vinaigrette.

4. About 10 minutes before the vegetables are done, cut steak in half crosswise (if it's one long piece) and rub with the remaining spice mixture. Heat the remaining 1 tablespoon oil in a large skillet over medium-high heat. Cook the steak, turning once, 2 to 3 minutes per side for medium-rare. Let rest on a clean cutting board for 5 minutes, then thinly slice against the grain.

5. Drizzle the roasted vegetables with the vinaigrette and serve with the steak.

SERVES 4: 3 oz. steak & 1¾ cups vegetables each

Calories 437 | Fat 24g (sat 6g) | Cholesterol 74mg | Carbohydrates 27g | Total sugars 9g (added 0g) | Protein 28g | Fiber 6g | Sodium 480mg | Potassium 1,257mg. Nutrition bonus: Vitamin A (336% daily value) | Vitamin C (76% dv) | Vitamin B$_{12}$ (71% dv) | Iron (22% dv) | Folate (20% dv).

all in one pot

At the end of a hectic day, sometimes the last thing you want to tackle is a sink full of dinner dishes. That's where cooking a meal all in one pot can be your best strategy. And while you might immediately think of soups and stews when you hear "one pot," there are all sorts of recipes that can be made in just one vessel.

This chapter includes casseroles, roasted dinners, salads and stir-fries. The trick is to try to get a bit of everything into the mix. In soups that's easy—use a little meat or beans for protein, whole grains and plenty of vegetables. With a sheet pan, try roasting your vegetables right alongside the chicken. You can even make a pasta dish in one pot, no extra boiling water required. See page 121 to find out how.

Braised Cauliflower &
Squash Penne Pasta
(page 121)

ACTIVE 40 min
TOTAL 40 min

To Make Ahead:
Refrigerate for up to 3 days or
freeze for up to 3 months.

quick beef & barley soup

Quick-cooking barley and sirloin steak help get this soup on the table swiftly—and the recipe doubles easily so, if you want, you can have plenty of leftovers. If the soup gets overly thick in the fridge, just add a little broth when you reheat it. Serve with crusty bread.

- **8 ounces sirloin steak, trimmed and cut into bite-size pieces**
- **1/2 teaspoon ground pepper, divided**
- **4 teaspoons extra-virgin olive oil, divided**
- **1 medium onion, chopped**
- **1 large stalk celery, sliced**
- **1 large carrot, sliced**
- **2 tablespoons tomato paste**
- **1 tablespoon chopped fresh thyme *or* 1 teaspoon dried**
- **3/4 cup quick barley**
- **4 cups reduced-sodium beef broth**
- **1 cup water**
- **1/4 teaspoon salt**
- **1-2 teaspoons red-wine vinegar**

1. Sprinkle steak with 1/4 teaspoon pepper. Heat 2 teaspoons oil in a large pot over medium heat. Add the steak and cook, stirring occasionally, until browned on all sides, about 2 minutes. Transfer to a bowl.

2. Add the remaining 2 teaspoons oil, onion and celery to the pot and cook, stirring, until beginning to soften, about 2 minutes. Add carrot and cook, stirring, for 2 minutes more. Add tomato paste and thyme and cook, stirring, until the vegetables are coated with the tomato paste and are beginning to brown, 1 to 2 minutes.

3. Add barley, broth, water, salt and the remaining 1/4 teaspoon pepper; bring to a simmer. Reduce heat to maintain a simmer and cook until the barley is tender, about 15 minutes. Return the beef and any accumulated juices to the pot and heat through, 1 to 2 minutes. Remove from the heat; stir in vinegar to taste.

SERVES 4: about 1 1/2 cups each

Calories 273 | Fat 9g (sat 2g) | Cholesterol 30mg | Carbohydrates 29g | Total sugars 4g (added 0g) | Protein 20g | Fiber 5g | Sodium 332mg | Potassium 647mg. **Nutrition bonus:** Vitamin A (65% daily value).

creamy turnip soup

In this recipe, the humble turnip is transformed into an elegant soup enriched with just 1 tablespoon of butter. It makes a great lunch or a satisfying but light supper, although you could also serve it in smaller portions as a starter. The salad on top gives the dish texture and a pop of flavor from the vinaigrette.

- **4** medium turnips (about 1$\frac{1}{2}$ pounds) plus 1$\frac{1}{2}$ cups thinly sliced turnip greens *or* spinach, divided
- **2** tablespoons extra-virgin olive oil, divided
- **1** tablespoon butter
- **1** medium onion, sliced
- $\frac{1}{2}$ teaspoon dried rosemary
- $\frac{1}{2}$ teaspoon salt plus a pinch, divided
- $\frac{1}{4}$ teaspoon ground white pepper plus a pinch, divided
- **4** cups low-sodium chicken broth
- $\frac{1}{4}$ cup shredded carrot
- **2** tablespoons thinly sliced scallion greens
- **2** teaspoons white-wine vinegar

1. Peel and slice turnips. Heat 1 tablespoon oil and butter in a large saucepan over medium heat. Add onion and cook, stirring, until beginning to brown, about 5 minutes. Add the turnips, rosemary, $\frac{1}{2}$ teaspoon salt and $\frac{1}{4}$ teaspoon white pepper; stir to combine. Cover and cook, stirring once or twice, for 10 minutes.

2. Add broth, increase heat to high and bring to a boil. Reduce heat to maintain a simmer, cover and cook until the turnips are tender, 10 to 12 minutes more.

3. Meanwhile, toss the turnip greens (or spinach) in a medium bowl with carrot, scallion greens, vinegar, the remaining 1 tablespoon oil and a pinch each of salt and pepper.

4. Puree the soup in the pan using an immersion blender or transfer to a regular blender and blend until smooth. (Use caution when pureeing hot liquids.) Serve the soup topped with some of the salad.

SERVES 4: about 1$\frac{1}{2}$ cups soup & generous $\frac{1}{4}$ cup salad each

Calories 188 | Fat 12g (sat 3g) | Cholesterol 8mg | Carbohydrates 17g | Total sugars 7g (added 0g) | Protein 7g | Fiber 4g | Sodium 506mg | Potassium 604mg. **Nutrition bonus:** Vitamin A & Vitamin C (73% daily value).

skillet swiss steak

This pan-fried Swiss steak takes only minutes but has all the flavor of a traditional hours-long braised version. Ask your butcher for 4 thin, equal-size cube steaks so they cook evenly. Sautéed peppers, onions and tomatoes make a savory sauce. *(Photo: page 6.)*

4 cube steaks (1-1¼ pounds total)

½ teaspoon salt, divided

¼ teaspoon ground pepper

¼ cup white whole-wheat flour

2 tablespoons extra-virgin olive oil, divided

1 large onion, cut into ½-inch-thick slices (don't separate)

1 medium green bell pepper, thinly sliced

1 clove garlic, minced

1 teaspoon chopped fresh thyme

1 14-ounce can whole tomatoes

1 tablespoon reduced-sodium soy sauce

1. Preheat oven to 200°F.

2. Sprinkle steaks with ¼ teaspoon salt and pepper. Place flour in a shallow dish and dredge the steaks in it.

3. Heat 1 tablespoon oil in a large skillet over medium-high heat. Reduce heat to medium and cook the steaks until browned, 2 to 4 minutes per side. Transfer to a baking sheet and keep warm in the oven.

4. Heat the remaining 1 tablespoon oil in the pan over medium-high heat. Add onion slices and cook, turning once and pressing with a spatula a few times, until browned on both sides, 4 to 6 minutes total. Stir in bell pepper, separating the onion rings as you stir, and cook, stirring occasionally, until the vegetables are tender, 3 to 4 minutes. Stir in garlic, thyme and the remaining ¼ teaspoon salt; cook, stirring, for 15 seconds. Add tomatoes with their juice and soy sauce. Cook, stirring, breaking up the tomatoes and scraping up any browned bits, until thickened, about 5 minutes. Serve the sauce over the steaks.

SERVES 4: 1 steak & ¾ cup sauce each

Calories 355 | **Fat** 16g (sat 4g) | **Cholesterol** 105mg | **Carbohydrates** 15g | **Total sugars** 4g (added 0g) | **Protein** 40g | **Fiber** 3g | **Sodium** 661mg | **Potassium** 320mg. **Nutrition bonus:** Vitamin C (66% daily value) | Iron (33% dv).

braised cauliflower & squash penne pasta

Cooking the pasta and vegetables in broth rather than water makes this vegetarian dish even more flavorful. And the starch from the pasta combines with the broth as it simmers to give the sauce body. Choose vegetarian "no-chicken" broth for its rich flavor and pale golden color instead of darker vegetable broth for this dish. *(Photo: page 114.)*

1 tablespoon extra-virgin olive oil

3 large cloves garlic, minced

1 teaspoon dried thyme

1/4 teaspoon crushed red pepper

4 cups "no-chicken" broth *or* vegetable broth

8 ounces whole-wheat penne

2 cups cauliflower florets (1-inch)

2 cups chopped peeled butternut squash (1-inch)

Ground pepper to taste

1/4 cup finely shredded Pecorino Romano cheese

Heat oil in a large saucepan over medium-high heat. Add garlic, thyme and crushed red pepper and cook, stirring, for 1 minute. Add broth, penne, cauliflower and squash. Bring to a boil over high heat. Reduce heat to maintain a lively simmer and cook, uncovered, until the pasta is tender and the liquid has thickened and greatly reduced, 14 to 16 minutes. Remove from heat, stir in pepper and let stand for 5 minutes. Serve topped with cheese.

SERVES 4: about 1 1/2 cups each

Calories 322 | **Fat** 7g (sat 2g) | **Cholesterol** 4mg | **Carbohydrates** 53g | **Total sugars** 5g (added 0g) | **Protein** 10g | **Fiber** 10g | **Sodium** 654mg | **Potassium** 472mg. **Nutrition bonus:** Vitamin A (136% daily value) | Vitamin C (52% dv).

chicken thighs
with couscous & kale

Boneless chicken thighs cook up fast, plus their slightly higher fat content makes them less prone to drying out than chicken breast. Look for whole-wheat pearl couscous, also known as Israeli couscous, in well-stocked supermarkets or specialty-foods stores.

1½ **teaspoons dried thyme**

1½ **teaspoons ground cumin**

¼ **teaspoon salt**

¼ **teaspoon ground pepper**

4 **large boneless, skinless chicken thighs (about 1¼ pounds), trimmed**

2 **tablespoons extra-virgin olive oil, divided**

1 **medium onion, halved and sliced**

1 **cup whole-wheat pearl couscous**

2 **cloves garlic, minced**

4 **cups very thinly sliced kale**

2 **cups reduced-sodium chicken broth**

1. Combine thyme, cumin, salt and pepper in a small bowl. Sprinkle both sides of chicken with half of the spice mixture.

2. Heat 1 tablespoon oil in a large cast-iron skillet over medium-high heat. Add the chicken and cook until golden brown, 2 to 3 minutes per side. Transfer to a plate.

3. Add the remaining 1 tablespoon oil and onion to the pan; cook, stirring frequently, until beginning to soften, 2 to 4 minutes. Stir in couscous and garlic; cook, stirring frequently, until the couscous is lightly toasted, 1 to 2 minutes. Add kale and the remaining spice mixture; cook, stirring, until the kale begins to wilt, 1 to 2 minutes.

4. Pour in broth and any accumulated juices from the chicken, then nestle the chicken into the couscous. Reduce the heat to medium-low, cover and cook until the chicken is cooked through and the couscous is tender, 15 to 18 minutes.

SERVES 4: 1 thigh & ¾ cup couscous each

Calories 409 | **Fat** 16g (sat 3g) | **Cholesterol** 76mg | **Carbohydrates** 37g | **Total sugars** 2g (added 0g) | **Protein** 29g | **Fiber** 4g | **Sodium** 494mg | **Potassium** 385mg. **Nutrition bonus:** Vitamin C (37% daily value) | Vitamin A (33% dv).

paprika chicken thighs
with brussels sprouts

Paprika-rubbed chicken thighs are nestled into Brussels sprouts and shallots and roasted on a sheet pan in the oven for an easy dinner. As the chicken thighs roast, the garlicky drippings flavor the Brussels sprouts and shallots—yum! Smoked paprika adds a touch of smoky flavor—look for it at well-stocked supermarkets or in the bulk-spice section at natural-foods markets. Regular paprika can be used in its place.

1 pound Brussels sprouts, trimmed and halved (or quartered if large)

4 small shallots, quartered

1 lemon, sliced

3 tablespoons extra-virgin olive oil, divided

3/4 teaspoon salt, divided

1/2 teaspoon ground pepper, divided

2 cloves garlic, minced

1 tablespoon smoked paprika, sweet *or* hot

1 teaspoon dried thyme

4 large *or* **8** small bone-in chicken thighs (about **2 1/2 pounds**), skin removed

1. Position rack in lower third of oven; preheat to 450°F.

2. Combine Brussels sprouts, shallots and lemon with 2 tablespoons oil and 1/4 teaspoon each salt and pepper on a large rimmed baking sheet.

3. Mash garlic and the remaining 1/2 teaspoon salt with the side of a chef's knife to form a paste. Combine the garlic paste with paprika, thyme and the remaining 1 tablespoon oil and 1/4 teaspoon pepper in a small bowl. Rub the paste all over chicken. Nestle the chicken into the Brussels sprouts.

4. Roast on the lower rack until the Brussels sprouts are tender and an instant-read thermometer inserted into the thickest part of the chicken without touching bone registers 165°F, 20 to 25 minutes.

SERVES 4: 1 large or 2 small thighs & 3/4 cup vegetables each

Calories 453 | **Fat** 25g (sat 5g) | **Cholesterol** 216mg | **Carbohydrates** 14g | **Total sugars** 3g (added 0g) | **Protein** 44g | **Fiber** 5g | **Sodium** 638mg | **Potassium** 949mg. **Nutrition bonus:** Vitamin C (141% daily value) | Vitamin A (41% dv) | Iron (24% dv) | Folate (22% dv).

cauliflower & kale frittata

This frittata is loaded with vegetables, cauliflower and kale, plus big flavor from thyme, smoked paprika and goat cheese. If you like, try other greens, like spinach or chard, in place of the kale. Serve with a fresh green salad with toasted walnuts and sherry vinaigrette.

2 tablespoons extra-virgin olive oil, divided

1 small onion, sliced

2 cups small cauliflower florets

¼ cup water

5 cups chopped kale

3 cloves garlic, minced

1 teaspoon chopped fresh thyme

½ teaspoon salt, divided

½ teaspoon ground pepper, divided

8 large eggs

½ teaspoon smoked paprika

½ cup crumbled goat cheese *or* shredded Manchego cheese

1. Position a rack in upper third of oven; preheat broiler to high.

2. Heat 1 tablespoon oil in a large cast-iron skillet over medium heat. Add onion and cook, stirring occasionally, until starting to brown, 2 to 4 minutes. Add cauliflower and water. Cover and cook until just tender, about 6 minutes. Add kale, garlic, thyme and ¼ teaspoon each salt and pepper; cook, stirring often, until the kale is wilted, 2 to 3 minutes.

3. Whisk eggs, paprika and the remaining ¼ teaspoon each salt and pepper in a large bowl. Add the vegetables to the egg mixture; gently stir to combine. Wipe the pan clean; add the remaining 1 tablespoon oil and heat over medium heat. Pour in the egg mixture and top with cheese. Cover and cook until the edges are set and the bottom is brown, 4 to 5 minutes.

4. Transfer the pan to the oven and broil until the top of the frittata is just cooked, 2 to 3 minutes.

SERVES 4: ¼ frittata each

Calories 293 | **Fat** 21g (sat 7g) | **Cholesterol** 383mg | **Carbohydrates** 8g | **Total sugars** 3g (added 0g) | **Protein** 18g | **Fiber** 2g | **Sodium** 517mg | **Potassium** 465mg. **Nutrition bonus:** Vitamin C (87% daily value) | Vitamin A (58% dv) | Folate (27% dv).

ACTIVE | 35 min
TOTAL | 35 min

To Make Ahead:
Refrigerate for up to
3 days or freeze for
up to 3 months.

middle eastern chicken & chickpea stew

This quick, protein-packed stew gets vibrant flavor from cumin, lemon juice and garlic. Make a double batch and freeze some for another night. Serve the stew over whole-wheat couscous with steamed broccoli on the side.

4 cloves garlic, finely chopped

3/4 teaspoon salt, divided

1/4 cup lemon juice

1 teaspoon ground cumin

1 teaspoon paprika

1/2 teaspoon ground pepper

1 pound boneless, skinless chicken breasts, trimmed, cut into 1-inch pieces

1 tablespoon extra-virgin olive oil

1 large yellow onion, chopped

1 14-ounce can no-salt-added diced tomatoes

1 15-ounce can chickpeas, rinsed

1/4 cup chopped flat-leaf parsley

1. Mash garlic and 1/2 teaspoon salt on a cutting board with the back of a fork until a paste forms. Transfer to a medium bowl and whisk in lemon juice, cumin, paprika and pepper. Add chicken and stir to coat.

2. Heat oil in a large cast-iron skillet over medium-high heat. Add onion and cook, stirring occasionally, until golden brown, 6 to 8 minutes. Using a slotted spoon, transfer the chicken to the pan (reserve the marinade) and cook, stirring occasionally, until opaque on the outside, about 4 minutes. Add tomatoes with their juice, chickpeas, the reserved marinade and the remaining 1/4 teaspoon salt. Reduce heat to medium and cook, stirring occasionally, until the chicken is cooked through, 5 to 7 minutes more. Serve sprinkled with parsley.

SERVES 4: 1 1/4 cups each

Calories 267 | **Fat** 8g (sat 1g) | **Cholesterol** 63mg | **Carbohydrates** 21g | **Total sugars** 4g (added 0g) | **Protein** 28g | **Fiber** 6g | **Sodium** 613mg | **Potassium** 554mg. **Nutrition bonus:** Vitamin C (45% daily value) | Vitamin A (21% dv).

cornbread-topped chili casserole

This riff on tamale pie features a robustly seasoned pork and vegetable filling and a simple buttermilk cornbread topping. Bake it in a cast-iron pan and take it directly from oven to table. For the best texture, use medium-grind yellow cornmeal. Serve with lime wedges.

4 **tablespoons canola oil, divided**

2 **cups chopped onion**

3 **tablespoons chili powder**

1 **pound lean ground pork** (*see Tip, page 247*)

2 **cups diced zucchini**

$^{1}/_{2}$ **teaspoon salt, divided**

$^{1}/_{2}$ **teaspoon ground pepper, divided**

2 **cups corn kernels, fresh** *or* **frozen (thawed)**

1 **14-ounce can diced tomatoes**

$1^{1}/_{2}$ **cups stone-ground cornmeal**

$^{3}/_{4}$ **teaspoon baking powder**

1 **large egg**

1 **cup buttermilk** (*see Tip*)

1. Preheat oven to 400°F.

2. Heat 2 tablespoons oil in a large cast-iron skillet over medium-high heat. Add onion and chili powder; cook, stirring, until starting to soften, about 2 minutes. Add pork, zucchini and $^{1}/_{4}$ teaspoon each salt and pepper; cook, stirring often, until pork is no longer pink, 4 to 5 minutes. Add corn and tomatoes with their juice and cook until heated through, 3 to 4 minutes more. Remove from heat.

3. Meanwhile, whisk cornmeal, baking powder and the remaining $^{1}/_{4}$ teaspoon each salt and pepper in a medium bowl. Whisk egg, buttermilk and the remaining 2 tablespoons oil in another bowl. Stir the buttermilk mixture into the cornmeal mixture until combined. Spread the batter over the pork and vegetables. Transfer the pan to the oven.

4. Bake until the cornbread is just cooked through, 15 to 20 minutes.

SERVES 5: about $1^{1}/_{2}$ cups each

Calories 490 | Fat 21g (sat 4g) | **Cholesterol** 92mg | **Carbohydrates** 55g | **Total sugars** 12g (added 0g) | **Protein** 28g | **Fiber** 8g | **Sodium** 749mg | **Potassium** 1,001mg. **Nutrition bonus:** Vitamin C (47% daily value) | Vitamin A (43% dv) | Iron (23% dv).

 *clean it up*

Some brands of buttermilk use stabilizers like carrageenan and mono- and diglycerides to help thicken the product and prevent separation. The Center for Science in the Public Interest (CSPI) deems mono- and diglycerides safe. However, some research shows carrageenan may cause digestive inflammation. Don't have buttermilk? To make a substitute, add 1 tablespoon lemon juice or vinegar to a cup of milk, let stand for 5 minutes and shake well.

ACTIVE 30 min

TOTAL 30 min

To Make Ahead:
Refrigerate sauce (Step 1)
for up to 3 days.

carrot, snow pea & chicken stir-fry

Stir-frying is an excellent way to use up a variety of vegetables you may have in the fridge. This recipe uses fresh snow peas and includes a citrusy mojo sauce. But any other vegetables you might like—broccoli florets, sliced bell peppers or carrots, sugar snap peas—all make great additions.

SAUCE

- ¼ **cup lime juice**
- ¼ **cup orange juice**
- ¼ **cup finely chopped fresh cilantro**
- 1 **tablespoon extra-virgin olive oil**
- 2 **teaspoons cornstarch**
- ¾ **teaspoon salt**
- ½ **teaspoon ground cumin**
- ½ **teaspoon dried oregano**
- ½ **teaspoon ground pepper**

STIR-FRY

- 3 **tablespoons peanut oil *or* canola oil, divided**
- 1 **pound boneless, skinless chicken thighs, trimmed, cut into 1-inch pieces**
- 3 **cups sliced carrots (½- to 1-inch pieces)**
- 1 **bunch scallions, trimmed, cut into 1-inch pieces**
- 3 **cloves garlic, minced**
- 3 **cups snow peas, trimmed**

1. **To prepare sauce:** Combine lime juice, orange juice, cilantro, olive oil, cornstarch, salt, cumin, oregano and pepper in a small bowl. Place near the stove.

2. **To prepare stir-fry:** Heat a 14-inch flat-bottom carbon-steel wok over high heat. (You'll know it's hot enough when a bead of water vaporizes within 1 to 2 seconds of contact.) Add 1 tablespoon oil and swirl to coat. Add chicken and stir-fry until just cooked, 2 to 4 minutes. Transfer to a large plate.

3. Swirl in another 1 tablespoon oil; add carrots and scallions. Stir-fry for 2 minutes.

4. Swirl in the remaining 1 tablespoon oil; add garlic and snow peas. Stir-fry until the vegetables are tender, 2 to 4 minutes more.

5. Return the chicken to the wok. Add the reserved sauce and cook, gently stirring, until well coated and hot, 1 to 2 minutes.

SERVES 4: 1½ cups each

Calories 356 | **Fat** 22g (sat 5g) | **Cholesterol** 76mg | **Carbohydrates** 16g | **Total sugars** 6g (added 0g) | **Protein** 24g | **Fiber** 4g | **Sodium** 541mg | **Potassium** 529mg. **Nutrition bonus:** Vitamin A (220% daily value) | Vitamin C (86% dv).

mom's chili

ACTIVE 45 min
TOTAL 2 1/4 hrs

To Make Ahead:
Refrigerate for up to 5 days
or freeze for up to 6 months.

Every cook should have an amazing chili recipe, and this one is both delicious and easy to make. Make a double batch, because it freezes really well. Serve topped with diced red onion, sliced scallions, shredded cheese and your favorite hot sauce.

1 tablespoon canola oil

3 cups finely chopped onions

2 cups finely chopped green bell peppers

1 clove garlic, minced

2 pounds lean ground beef (90% *or* leaner)

1 cup water

1 14-ounce can no-salt-added diced tomatoes

1 6-ounce can tomato paste

2 bay leaves

1/4 cup chili powder

1 teaspoon ground cumin

1 teaspoon red-wine vinegar

3/4 teaspoon salt

Ground pepper to taste

Pinch of cayenne pepper

1 15-ounce can kidney beans, rinsed

1. Heat oil in a large pot over medium-high heat. Add onions, bell peppers and garlic and cook, stirring frequently, until tender, about 15 minutes. Add beef and cook, breaking it up with a spoon, until no longer pink, 7 to 8 minutes. Add water, tomatoes and their juice, tomato paste, bay leaves, chili powder, cumin, vinegar, salt, pepper and cayenne; stir well to combine. Cover and simmer over low heat for 1 hour.

2. Stir in beans and cook, uncovered, for 30 minutes more. Remove bay leaves before serving

SERVES 8: generous 1 cup each

Calories 303 | Fat 12g (sat 4g) | Cholesterol 72mg | Carbohydrates 23g | Total sugars 7g (added 0g) | Protein 27g | Fiber 8g | Sodium 674mg | Potassium 940mg. Nutrition bonus: Vitamin C (77% daily value) | Vitamin A (38% dv) | Vitamin B_{12} (35% dv) | Iron (27% dv).

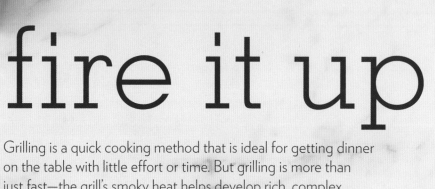

fire it up

Grilling is a quick cooking method that is ideal for getting dinner on the table with little effort or time. But grilling is more than just fast—the grill's smoky heat helps develop rich, complex flavors in what could otherwise be standard fare. Unfortunately, compounds in that smoke—particularly when it comes from fat drippings burning on hot coals and then wafting back onto food—have been linked to certain types of cancers. But experts say that compared to other cancer risks, this one is minimal. Still, if you want to be safer, trim excess fat from meat and poultry, avoid cooking directly over open flames (like a campfire or fiery charcoal) and try to control flare-ups. With all this in mind, we still turn to this essential tool on a regular basis. Our recipes use bold spices and rubs, tangy homemade marinades, from-scratch sauces and vegetable- and fruit-based salsas as simple ways to enhance, but not overpower, the great flavor the grill offers.

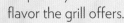

Pork Fajitas with
Smoky Cherry Salsa
(page 159)

sesame-ginger pork patty with grilled pineapple

Ditch the bun and serve this Asian-inspired pork burger with sweet grilled pineapple on top of a zesty watercress-and-carrot salad. We like the taste and texture of fresh pineapple for this recipe, but canned pineapple rings work well too. Serve with short-grain brown rice.

3 tablespoons reduced-sodium soy sauce

2 scallions, chopped

2 cloves garlic, minced

1 tablespoon minced fresh ginger

2 teaspoons sesame oil, divided

1 pound ground pork *(see Tip, page 247)*

1 tablespoon rice vinegar

4 pineapple rings, ¼ inch thick

4 cups watercress (about 1 large bunch), tough stems removed

1 cup shredded carrot

1. Preheat grill to medium-high.

2. Combine soy sauce, scallions, garlic, ginger and 1 teaspoon sesame oil in a small bowl.

3. Place pork in a medium bowl. Add half of the sauce mixture to the pork and gently combine without overmixing. Form into 4 patties, about ¾ inch thick. Add the remaining 1 teaspoon sesame oil and vinegar to the remaining sauce mixture and set aside.

4. Dip a folded paper towel in a little oil, hold it with tongs and rub it over the grill rack. Grill the burgers, turning once, until an instant-read thermometer inserted in the center registers 155°F, 4 to 5 minutes per side. During the last 3 minutes of cooking, add the pineapple rings to the grill and cook, turning once, until dark grill marks appear.

5. Combine watercress and carrot in a large bowl. Toss with 2 tablespoons of the reserved sauce. Divide the salad among 4 plates. Top each portion with a pineapple ring and a burger. Drizzle any remaining sauce on top.

SERVES 4: 1 patty (3 oz.) & about 1 cup salad each

Calories 217 | Fat 9g (sat 3g) | **Cholesterol** 66mg | **Carbohydrates** 13g | **Total sugars** 7g (added 0g) | **Protein** 25g | **Fiber** 2g | **Sodium** 531mg | **Potassium** 540mg. **Nutrition bonus:** Vitamin A (116% daily value) | Vitamin C (75% dv).

spicy tunisian grilled chicken

ACTIVE 5 min
TOTAL 25 min

To Make Ahead:
Store spice mixture (Step 1) in an airtight container for up to 3 months; coat chicken with it up to 30 minutes before grilling.

Freshly ground coriander, caraway and crushed red pepper give this grilled chicken a kick, but if you prefer your food less spicy, simply cut back on the red pepper. Try it on grilled pork tenderloin or meaty salmon steaks too.

2 **teaspoons coriander seeds**

2 **teaspoons caraway seeds**

³/₄ **teaspoon crushed red pepper**

³/₄ **teaspoon garlic powder**

¹/₂ **teaspoon kosher salt**

1-1¹/₄ **pounds boneless, skinless chicken breast**

1. Grind coriander seeds, caraway seeds and crushed red pepper in a spice grinder (or clean coffee grinder or mortar and pestle) until finely ground. Transfer to a small bowl and stir in garlic powder and salt.

2. Coat both sides of chicken with the spice mixture up to 30 minutes before grilling.

3. Preheat grill to medium-high.

4. Dip a folded paper towel in a little oil, hold it with tongs and rub it over the grill rack. Grill the chicken, turning once, until an instant-read thermometer inserted into the thickest part registers 165°F, 4 to 8 minutes per side.

SERVES 4: 4 oz. each

Calories 131 | **Fat** 3g (sat 1g) | **Cholesterol** 63mg | **Carbohydrates** 2g | **Total sugars** 0g (added 0g) | **Protein** 23g | **Fiber** 1g | **Sodium** 195mg | **Potassium** 228mg.

ACTIVE 1 hr
TOTAL 1 hr (plus
marinating time)

To Make Ahead:
Prepare through Step 1
up to 1 day ahead.

chimichurri grilled steak salad

Chimichurri is a zingy sauce from Argentina made with garlic, parsley, vinegar and olive oil. Here, it doubles as a marinade for flank steak and as a dressing for the accompanying salad.

1 cup packed flat-leaf parsley
5 tablespoons extra-virgin olive oil, divided
¼ cup white vinegar
1 small clove garlic, chopped
¾ teaspoon salt, divided
1 pound flank steak, trimmed
2 hearts *or* small heads of romaine
1 large bell pepper, quartered
1 small red onion, sliced ½ inch thick

1. Puree parsley, 1 tablespoon oil, vinegar, garlic and ¼ teaspoon salt in a blender. Pat 1 tablespoon of the mixture on each side of steak. Put the steak on a plate, cover and refrigerate for at least 1 hour and up to 24 hours. Add 3 tablespoons oil to the herb mixture remaining in the blender; pulse to blend. Transfer to a bowl, cover and refrigerate if not using right away.

2. Twenty minutes before you are ready to grill, preheat grill to medium-high.

3. Cut each heart (or head) of romaine in half lengthwise, leaving the root end intact. Brush lettuce, bell pepper and onion with the remaining

1 tablespoon oil. Sprinkle with ¼ teaspoon salt. Sprinkle the steak with the remaining ¼ teaspoon salt. Let the dressing come to room temperature, if necessary, while you grill.

4. Dip a folded paper towel in a little oil, hold it with tongs and rub it over the grill rack. Grill the steak, turning once, until desired doneness, 6 to 8 minutes per side for medium. Grill the pepper and onion, turning occasionally, until charred and tender, about 10 minutes total. Grill the lettuce, turning once, until lightly charred, about 2 minutes per side.

5. Let the steak rest on a clean cutting board for 5 minutes, then thinly slice against the grain. Slice the bell pepper and separate the onion into rings. Divide the lettuce, steak, pepper and onion among 4 plates. Drizzle with the reserved dressing.

SERVES 4: 3 oz. steak each

Calories 363 | **Fat** 24g (sat 5g) | **Cholesterol** 70mg | **Carbohydrates** 9g | **Total sugars** 4g (added 0g) | **Protein** 27g | **Fiber** 4g | **Sodium** 518mg | **Potassium** 864mg. **Nutrition bonus:** Vitamin A (248% daily value) | Vitamin C (131% dv) | Folate (53% dv) | Iron (22% dv) | Vitamin B$_{12}$ (20% dv).

grilled portobellos
with chopped salad

Earthy, marinated mushrooms are the star of this meatless meal and make an ideal base for a colorful array of grilled veggies mixed with white beans, lemon and dill. Melted fontina cheese has a delicious nuttiness to it, but Cheddar would work well too.

- ¼ cup lemon juice
- 3 tablespoons extra-virgin olive oil
- ¼ cup chopped fresh dill
- 3 cloves garlic, minced
- ½ teaspoon salt
- ½ teaspoon ground pepper
- 4 large portobello mushroom caps, gills removed
- 1 15-ounce can small white beans, rinsed
- 2 small bell peppers, quartered and seeded
- 1 small red onion, cut into ¼-inch-thick slices
- 1 medium zucchini, cut lengthwise into ¼-inch slices
- 1 cup shredded fontina cheese

1. Preheat grill to medium-high.

2. Combine lemon juice, oil, dill, garlic, salt and pepper in a large bowl. Add mushroom caps and turn to coat. Remove the mushrooms from the bowl. Add white beans; stir to coat.

3. Place the mushroom caps gill-side up on the grill with peppers, onion and zucchini. Grill the vegetables, turning once, until they start to char and soften, about 8 minutes for the mushrooms and 6 minutes for the other vegetables. Turn the mushrooms gill-side up again. Fill each with ¼ cup cheese and grill until the cheese is melted, about 1 minute more.

4. Chop peppers, onion and zucchini and add to the bowl with the beans; toss to combine. Top each mushroom with about 1 cup of the grilled salad.

SERVES 4: 1 mushroom cap & about 1 cup salad each

Calories 312 | Fat 20g (sat 7g) | Cholesterol 31mg | Carbohydrates 25g | Total sugars 7g (added 0g) | Protein 15g | Fiber 7g | Sodium 736mg | Potassium 850mg. Nutrition bonus: Vitamin C (107% daily value) | Folate (34% dv) | Vitamin A (31% dv) | Calcium (22% dv).

ACTIVE : 30 min
TOTAL : 30 min

Equipment:
4 (12-inch) skewers

curried shrimp & potato kebabs

A flavor-packed marinade made from curry powder, garlic and cilantro amps up these baby potato and shrimp kebabs, which cook quickly on the grill. Don't skip the creamy yogurt-lime dipping sauce to serve alongside.

12 new *or* baby potatoes

3 tablespoons canola oil

2 tablespoons chopped fresh cilantro

1 tablespoon curry powder *(see Tip)*

3 cloves garlic, minced

1/4 teaspoon salt

20 peeled and deveined raw shrimp, tails left on (20-25 per pound)

1/2 cup nonfat plain yogurt

1 teaspoon lime juice

1. Preheat grill to medium.

2. Place potatoes in a microwave-safe container. Cover and microwave on High until just tender when pierced with a fork, 3 to 3 1/2 minutes.

3. Meanwhile, combine oil, cilantro, curry powder, garlic and salt in a large bowl. Reserve 2 tablespoons of the mixture in a small bowl. Add shrimp and the potatoes to the large bowl; toss to coat. Thread the shrimp and potatoes onto four 12-inch skewers.

4. Grill the kebabs, turning once, until the shrimp are pink and the potatoes are browned, 2 to 3 minutes per side.

5. Stir yogurt and lime juice into the small bowl of reserved sauce. Serve each kebab with 2 tablespoons sauce.

SERVES 4: 1 kebab & 2 Tbsp. sauce each

Calories 246 | Fat 12g (sat 1g) | Cholesterol 143mg | Carbohydrates 15g | Total sugars 2g (added 0g) | Protein 19g | Fiber 2g | Sodium 342mg | Potassium 237mg. Nutrition bonus: Vitamin B_{12} (24% daily value) | Vitamin C (23% dv).

clean it up

Curry powder and other ground spices often contain silicon dioxide to help keep them dry, clump-free and easy to pour. The FDA and other watchdog groups say synthetic silicon dioxide is safe. But because it is super-small (called nanoparticles), some scientists say it could get into your bloodstream and have a different effect on your body than larger particles. Some research that suggests this additive could subtly impact your gut health. If you're concerned, choose organic, as silicon dioxide is banned in organics.

turkey kofta
with tahini sauce

ACTIVE 25 min
TOTAL 25 min

Equipment:
4 (10- to 12-inch)
flat metal skewers

Kofta is the common term for the combination of ground meat, onions and spices shaped into balls and cooked. These kofta kebabs of ground turkey and minced onion mixed with cumin and allspice make a delicious grilled dinner. Look for tahini alongside Middle Eastern ingredients or in the natural-foods section of the supermarket.

1 **pound 93%-lean ground turkey**

$^1/_2$ **cup minced onion**

$^1/_2$ **cup coarse fresh whole-wheat breadcrumbs** *(see Tip, page 247)*

5 **tablespoons chopped fresh cilantro, divided**

1 **teaspoon ground cumin, divided**

$^1/_2$ **teaspoon ground allspice**

$^1/_2$ **teaspoon salt plus** $^1/_8$ **teaspoon, divided**

$^1/_4$ **teaspoon cayenne pepper**

$^1/_3$ **cup low-fat plain yogurt**

2 **tablespoons tahini**

1 **tablespoon lemon juice**

1. Preheat grill to medium-high.

2. Combine turkey, onion, breadcrumbs, 4 tablespoons cilantro, $^1/_2$ teaspoon cumin, allspice, $^1/_2$ teaspoon salt and cayenne in a large bowl; gently knead together. Do not overmix. With damp hands, form the mixture into two ovals on each of 4 skewers; use about $^1/_3$ cup for each and place at least 1 inch apart.

3. Dip a folded paper towel in a little oil, hold it with tongs and rub it over the grill rack. Grill the kebabs until an instant-read thermometer inserted in the center registers 165°F, about 4 minutes per side.

4. Combine yogurt, tahini, lemon juice, the remaining 1 tablespoon cilantro, $^1/_2$ teaspoon cumin and $^1/_8$ teaspoon salt in a small bowl. Serve the kebabs with the sauce.

SERVES 4: 2 kofta & 2 Tbsp. sauce each

Calories 271 | Fat 14g (sat 3g) | Cholesterol 85mg | Carbohydrates 11g | Total sugars 3g (added 0g) | Protein 26g | Fiber 2g | Sodium 519mg | Potassium 401mg. Nutrition bonus: Vitamin B_{12} (25% daily value).

To Make Ahead:
Marinate chicken (Step 1)
for up to 8 hours.

yogurt-curry marinated chicken thighs

Marinating chicken in seasoned yogurt leaves it tender, juicy and infused with flavor. The marinade also works well with pork, shrimp, firm white fish or tofu. Serve with whole-wheat naan and grilled cauliflower.

1 cup nonfat plain yogurt

⅓ cup grated onion (about 1 medium)

3 tablespoons curry powder

1 tablespoon extra-virgin olive oil

1 teaspoon salt

½ teaspoon crushed red pepper

4 large *or* **8** small bone-in chicken thighs (about 2 pounds), skin removed

1. Whisk yogurt, onion, curry powder, oil, salt and crushed red pepper in a shallow pan. Add chicken and turn until well coated. Cover and refrigerate for at least 4 hours and up to 8 hours.

2. Preheat grill to medium-high or broiler to high. Remove chicken from marinade (discard marinade) and grill or broil, turning once or twice, until no longer pink in the center, 25 to 30 minutes.

SERVES 4: 1 large or 2 small thighs each

Calories 295 | Fat 15g (sat 4g) | Cholesterol 115mg | Carbohydrates 5g | Total sugars 3g (added 0g) | Protein 34g | Fiber 1g | Sodium 412mg | Potassium 360mg.

ACTIVE | 40 min
TOTAL | 2 hrs 50 min
(including 2 hrs
marinating time)

To Make Ahead:
Marinate chicken (Step 1)
for up to 8 hours.

grilled chicken
with blueberry-lime salsa

Lime adds a citrusy punch to simple grilled chicken breasts. We grate the zest into a quick rub that adds loads of flavor, then combine the lime segments with blueberries for a tart and refreshing salsa. Add more chile pepper if you like it spicy.

1 lime

1 tablespoon canola oil

1/4 teaspoon salt plus 1/8 teaspoon, divided

1/4 teaspoon ground pepper

2 bone-in, skinless chicken breasts, cut in half crosswise

1 cup blueberries, fresh *or* frozen (thawed), coarsely chopped if large

1/2 serrano *or* jalapeño pepper, or to taste, finely chopped

2 tablespoons finely chopped shallot

1 tablespoon chopped fresh cilantro

1. Zest lime (reserve the fruit). Combine the zest, oil, 1/4 teaspoon salt and pepper in a small bowl. Place chicken in a shallow dish meat-side up and spoon the zest mixture on top. Cover and refrigerate for at least 2 hours and up to 8 hours.

2. Preheat grill to medium.

3. Dip a folded paper towel in a little oil, hold it with tongs and rub it over the grill rack. Grill the chicken until an instant-read thermometer inserted in the thickest part without touching bone registers 165°F, 8 to 12 minutes per side. Transfer to a serving plate; let rest for 5 minutes.

4. Meanwhile, slice ends off the reserved lime. With a sharp knife, remove the white pith and discard. Cut lime segments from their surrounding membranes and coarsely chop. Combine in a small bowl with blueberries, chile pepper, shallot, cilantro and the remaining 1/8 teaspoon salt, stirring gently. Serve with the chicken.

SERVES 4: 1/2 chicken breast & about 1/4 cup salsa each

Calories 193 | Fat 7g (sat 1g) | Cholesterol 68mg | Carbohydrates 8g | Total sugars 4g (added 0g) | Protein 25g | Fiber 2g | Sodium 279mg | Potassium 274mg.

apple & grilled chicken salad with cheddar toasts

This hearty salad with melty cheese toasts highlights the classic combination of sharp Cheddar and sweet, crunchy apples. Skip the chicken and the salad becomes a fabulous starter or side.

- **1 pound boneless, skinless chicken breasts, trimmed**
- **³/4 teaspoon kosher salt, divided**
- **¹/2 teaspoon ground pepper, divided**
- **4 diagonal slices whole-wheat baguette (1 inch thick)**
- **¹/2 cup shredded aged Cheddar cheese**
- **3 tablespoons grapeseed oil *or* canola oil**
- **2 tablespoons cider vinegar**
- **1 tablespoon whole-grain mustard**
- **1 head escarole (about 1 pound), torn into bite-size pieces**
- **3 cups sliced sweet, crunchy apples (about 2 medium), such as Honeycrisp**
- **¹/4 cup slivered red onion**

1. Preheat grill to medium-high.

2. Sprinkle chicken with ¹/2 teaspoon salt and ¹/4 teaspoon pepper.

3. Dip a folded paper towel in a little oil, hold it with tongs and rub it over the grill rack. Grill the chicken, turning occasionally, until an instant-read thermometer inserted into the thickest part registers 165°F, about 15 minutes total. Grill baguette slices over the coolest part of the grill until toasted on the bottom, 1 to 3 minutes. Turn over, sprinkle with cheese and cook until the cheese melts, 1 to 3 minutes.

4. Meanwhile, whisk oil, vinegar, mustard and the remaining ¹/4 teaspoon each salt and pepper in a large bowl. Add escarole, apples and onion; toss to coat.

5. Slice the chicken. Divide the salad among 4 plates, top each with some chicken and serve with the cheese toasts.

SERVES 4: 3 cups salad, 3 oz. chicken & 1 toast each

Calories 420 | **Fat** 19g (sat 5g) | **Cholesterol** 77mg | **Carbohydrates** 33g | **Total sugars** 11g (added 0g) | **Protein** 30g | **Fiber** 6g | **Sodium** 619mg | **Potassium** 673mg. **Nutrition bonus:** Vitamin A (53% daily value) | Folate (43% dv) | Vitamin C (23% dv).

clean it up

Even bread that doesn't taste sweet or salty can have surprisingly amounts of added sugars and/or salt. Check the labels and choose brands that contain no more than 200 mg of sodium per slice and have no sugars in the ingredient list. In-store bakeries aren't necessarily any better than packaged brands—check those ingredients and labels too.

To Make Ahead:
Refrigerate dressing and
store croutons in an airtight
container at room temperature
for up to 3 days.

grilled salmon with
watercress salad & buttermilk dressing

Fresh watercress salad tossed with rich dill-infused buttermilk dressing creates the base for this grilled salmon dish. Most supermarkets sell fresh sauerkraut in the refrigerated section; if you can't find purple sauerkraut, feel free to use green (or make your own!).

CROUTONS

2 cups cubed whole-wheat bread (^{1}/2-inch)

1 teaspoon extra-virgin olive oil

BUTTERMILK DRESSING

^{1}/3 cup buttermilk

3 tablespoons mayonnaise

1 tablespoon cider vinegar

1 tablespoon chopped fresh dill

1 teaspoon Dijon mustard

1 small clove garlic, minced

^{1}/4 teaspoon fine sea salt

Hot sauce to taste

SALMON & SALAD

1 pound wild salmon, skin-on, cut into 4 portions

^{1}/4 teaspoon fine sea salt

^{1}/4 teaspoon ground pepper

8 cups gently packed trimmed watercress

^{1}/2 cup fresh sauerkraut, preferably purple

1. **To prepare croutons:** Preheat oven to 350°F. Toss bread and oil in a medium bowl. Spread on a rimmed baking sheet. Bake until crisp, 10 to 15 minutes.

2. Meanwhile, preheat grill to high.

3. **To prepare dressing:** Whisk buttermilk, mayonnaise, vinegar, dill, mustard, garlic, ^{1}/4 teaspoon salt and a couple dashes of hot sauce in a small bowl.

4. **To prepare salmon:** Season salmon with salt and pepper. Dip a folded paper towel in a little oil, hold it with tongs and rub it over the grill rack. Grill the salmon, skin-side down and without turning, until just cooked through, 3 to 6 minutes, depending on thickness. Transfer to a clean plate and tent with foil to keep warm.

5. Toss watercress with half of the dressing. Serve the salmon on the salad, garnished with sauerkraut and the croutons. Serve the remaining dressing on the side.

SERVES 4: 3 oz. salmon & 2 cups salad each

Calories 278 | Fat 14g (sat 3g) | **Cholesterol** 58mg | **Carbohydrates** 10g | **Total sugars** 3g (added 1g) | **Protein** 26g | **Fiber** 2g | **Sodium** 545mg | **Potassium** 637mg. **Nutrition bonus:** Vitamin B$_{12}$ (81% daily value) | Vitamin C (24% dv) | Vitamin A (22% dv).

grilled salmon
with tomatoes & basil

This dish is so beautiful and yet so simple to prepare—it's great for entertaining. Depending on how your salmon was prepared at the market, you may need to remove the small white pin bones in the fillet. To do so, place your hand under the fillet to bend it up so the bones poke out of the flesh. Grasp each bone with a clean pair of tweezers or needle-nose pliers and gently pull it out in the direction of the wide end of the fillet. (Photo: page 2.)

2 cloves garlic, minced

1 teaspoon kosher salt, divided

1 tablespoon extra-virgin olive oil

1 whole wild salmon fillet (also called a "side of salmon," about 1$\frac{1}{2}$ pounds)

$\frac{1}{3}$ cup plus $\frac{1}{4}$ cup thinly sliced fresh basil, divided

2 medium tomatoes, thinly sliced

$\frac{1}{4}$ teaspoon ground pepper

1. Preheat grill to medium.

2. Mash minced garlic and $\frac{3}{4}$ teaspoon salt on a cutting board with the side of a chef's knife or a spoon until a paste forms. Transfer to a small bowl and stir in oil.

3. Check salmon for pin bones and remove if necessary. Measure out a piece of heavy-duty foil (or use a double layer of regular foil) large enough for the salmon fillet. Coat the foil with cooking spray. Place the salmon skin-side down on the foil and spread the garlic mixture all over it. Sprinkle with $\frac{1}{3}$ cup basil. Overlap tomato slices on top and sprinkle with the remaining $\frac{1}{4}$ teaspoon salt and pepper.

4. Transfer the salmon on the foil to the grill. Grill until the fish flakes easily, 10 to 12 minutes. Use two large spatulas to slide the salmon from the foil to a serving platter. Serve the salmon sprinkled with the remaining $\frac{1}{4}$ cup basil.

SERVES 4: about 5 oz. each

Calories 248 | Fat 10g (sat 2g) | Cholesterol 80mg | Carbohydrates 3g | Total sugars 2g (added 0g) | Protein 35g | Fiber 1g | Sodium 367mg | Potassium 799mg. Nutrition bonus: Vitamin B$_{12}$ (121% daily value) | Vitamin A (22% dv) | Vitamin C (20% dv).

pork fajitas
with smoky cherry salsa

ACTIVE | 45 min
TOTAL | 45 min

To Make Ahead:
Marinate pork (Step 2) in the refrigerator, loosely covered, for up to 8 hours.

Chipotle peppers give this cherry salsa a touch of sweet heat. It's terrific for topping fajitas made from tender grilled pork tenderloin, onions and peppers. Manchego cheese, although not traditional for fajitas, adds a nice flavor layer to this dish. *(Photo: page 136.)*

1	teaspoon plus a pinch of salt, divided
2	cloves garlic, minced
	Zest of 2 limes
6	teaspoons lime juice, divided
1¼	teaspoons ground chipotle pepper, divided
1¼	pounds pork tenderloin, trimmed
1	medium white onion, thickly sliced crosswise
1	red *or* green bell pepper, quartered
1	cup chopped pitted sweet *or* sour fresh cherries (*see Tip, page 247*)
¼	cup finely chopped fresh cilantro
½	cup shredded Manchego *or* Cheddar cheese
8	6-inch corn tortillas, warmed

1. Preheat grill to medium-high.

2. Mash 1 teaspoon salt and garlic in a mortar and pestle (or in a small bowl with a spoon) until a paste forms. Mix in lime zest, 2 teaspoons lime juice and 1 teaspoon ground chipotle. Rub the paste all over pork.

3. Dip a folded paper towel in a little oil, hold it with tongs and rub it over the grill rack. Grill the pork, turning occasionally, until an instant-read thermometer inserted in the thickest part reaches 145°F, 13 to 15 minutes. Grill onion and bell pepper, turning occasionally, until charred and tender, 8 to 10 minutes. Transfer the pork to a clean cutting board and let rest for 5 minutes.

4. Combine cherries, cilantro, the remaining 4 teaspoons lime juice, the remaining ¼ teaspoon chipotle and pinch of salt in a bowl. Finely chop one slice of grilled onion and stir it into the salsa.

5. Thinly slice the remaining onion and pepper. Thinly slice the pork. Serve the pork and vegetables with the salsa and cheese on tortillas.

SERVES 4: 2 fajitas each

Calories 356 | **Fat** 10g (sat 4g) | **Cholesterol** 89mg | **Carbohydrates** 33g | **Total sugars** 7g (added 0g) | **Protein** 34g | **Fiber** 6g | **Sodium** 878mg | **Potassium** 744mg. **Nutrition bonus:** Vitamin C (88% daily value) | Vitamin A (38% dv).

so-simple sides

Having an arsenal of inspiring side dishes to choose from makes it easy to create a healthful meal. The idea here is to start with a few versatile, flexible recipes, like Greek Potato Salad *(page 172)*, Brown Rice Pilaf *(page 162)* and Asparagus Tabbouleh *(page 165)*. Then start swapping ingredients to create your own variations—we've given a few riffs to get you started. Mastering some of these go-to sides makes planning and cooking a complete meal a breeze. In addition, for those times when a recipe is not what you want, we've included basic cooking and seasoning instructions for all sorts of vegetables and grains *(starting on page 173)*. Your entree will never feel lonely again.

Greek Potato Salad (*page 172*)

brown rice pilaf

Brown rice doesn't have to be boring, especially when you turn it into a pilaf that's just as easy to make as boiling rice! Dried currants and toasty almonds give it a Mediterranean flair.

2 teaspoons extra-virgin olive oil

²/₃ cup long-grain brown rice

1¹/₃ cups water

¹/₄ cup currants

¹/₄ cup slivered *or* sliced almonds, toasted (*see Tip, page 247*)

Heat oil in a large saucepan over medium heat. Add rice and stir until starting to brown, about 3 minutes. Add water and bring to a boil. Reduce heat to maintain a low simmer, cover and cook until the rice is tender, 30 to 40 minutes. Remove from heat and let stand, covered, for 10 minutes. Fluff with a fork and toss with currants and almonds.

SERVES 4: about ²/₃ cup each

Calories 199 | Fat 7g (sat 1g) | Cholesterol 0mg | Carbohydrates 32g | Total sugars 7g (added 0g) | Protein 4g | Fiber 3g | Sodium 8mg | Potassium 175mg.

Simple Swaps

- Try red or black rice—which are also whole grains—or an aromatic variety, such as brown basmati. Adjust cooking times as necessary.

- Infuse this pilaf with deeper flavors by using beef, chicken or vegetable broth as the cooking liquid. You could even use fruit juice to take the taste in a sweeter direction.

- Instead of tossing in dried fruit and nuts, you could add chopped fresh vegetables or fruit for crunch. Or for a different texture, stir in your favorite chopped greens, like baby spinach, kale or escarole.

ACTIVE | 20 min
TOTAL | 1 hr 40 min

To Make Ahead:
Refrigerate, without feta,
for up to 8 hours.

asparagus tabbouleh

Asparagus has a short window when it's in season, so make this take on tabbouleh when it's in season in your area. The rest of the year choose whatever's best—traditional parsley or even Brussels sprouts or cabbage (as in the variations below). Serve with chicken kebabs, tzatziki and whole-wheat pita bread for a Middle Eastern–inspired dinner.

1/2 cup bulgur

8 ounces asparagus, trimmed, very finely chopped

1 cup pomegranate seeds

3/4 cup finely chopped fresh parsley

1/4 cup finely diced red onion

1/4 cup lemon juice

1/4 cup extra-virgin olive oil

1/2 teaspoon kosher salt

1/2 cup crumbled feta cheese, preferably Bulgarian

Simple Swaps

- Bulgur is the traditional grain for this parsley salad, but feel free to use cooked freekeh, barley, couscous or wild rice.

- No asparagus? Try chopped Brussels sprouts, snow peas or red cabbage instead.

- Skip the pomegranate seeds and go with golden raisins, chopped dried apricots or dates, or even goji berries for a pretty pink accent.

1. Place bulgur in a medium bowl and cover with several inches of cold water. Let soak for 1 hour. Drain.

2. Combine the bulgur, asparagus, pomegranate seeds, parsley, onion, lemon juice, oil and salt in a large nonreactive bowl (see Tip, page 247). Let stand at room temperature for 20 minutes or refrigerate for up to 8 hours. Serve topped with feta.

SERVES 6: 3/4 cup each

Calories 193 | Fat 13g (sat 3g) | Cholesterol 11mg | Carbohydrates 17g | Total sugars 5g (added 0g) | Protein 4g | Fiber 3g | Sodium 218mg | Potassium 228mg. Nutrition bonus: Vitamin C (31% daily value).

roasted carrots
with garlic confit & thyme

Browning carrots on the stovetop and then roasting them with butter, garlic oil and thyme in a hot oven brings out their earthy sweetness. You will end up with extra garlic oil from this recipe. Use it in a vinaigrette or to season other cooked vegetables.

½ **cup medium garlic cloves (about 16), unpeeled**

1 **cup extra-virgin olive oil**

30 **small carrots (about the diameter of a finger), scrubbed**

1 **teaspoon Maldon *or* other flaky sea salt**

1 **tablespoon unsalted butter**

4 **fresh thyme sprigs**

1 **teaspoon lemon juice**

1. Put garlic in a small saucepan and add enough oil to just cover it. Place over medium heat. Wait until you hear a quiet sizzle, then reduce heat to low. Cook, stirring occasionally, until the garlic is very soft, 30 to 45 minutes. Transfer the garlic with a slotted spoon to a small bowl and measure out 2 tablespoons of the garlic-infused oil. (Reserve the remaining oil for up to 1 month; use in salad dressing or to coat vegetables for roasting or grilling.)

2. Meanwhile, preheat oven to 500°F.

3. If your carrots have greens attached, trim off all but ½ inch of them. Add the 2 tablespoons garlic oil to a large ovenproof skillet and place over medium-high heat. When the oil is shimmering, add the carrots and sprinkle with salt.

Cook, gently turning occasionally, until browned in spots, 3 to 4 minutes. Add butter and let it melt, then toss with the carrots. Add the garlic cloves, skins and all, and thyme. Transfer the pan to the oven.

4. Roast, stirring once halfway through, until the carrots are evenly tender, 10 to 15 minutes. Drizzle with lemon juice. Serve the carrots with the garlic cloves, squeezing the soft garlic from the skins as you eat.

SERVES 4: 1 cup each

Calories 190 | **Fat** 13g (sat 3g) | **Cholesterol** 8mg | **Carbohydrates** 17g | **Total sugars** 7g (added 0g) | **Protein** 2g | **Fiber** 4g | **Sodium** 378mg | **Potassium** 497mg. **Nutrition bonus:** Vitamin A (117% daily value) | Vitamin C (21% dv).

Simple Swaps

- Almost any roasted root—or a blend of them—can shine in this side dish. Try parsnips, beets, baby turnips or something starchier like fingerling potatoes.

- Switch up your savory flavor by roasting sliced leeks, quartered shallots or cipollini onions instead of garlic.

- Try a different herb, such as rosemary or lavender.

sugar snap pea salad

Radishes, mint and creamy sheep's- or goat's-milk cheese add richness, texture and flavor to this dish. Crushed dried Aleppo pepper adds moderate heat with a hint of fruity tang; find it in specialty markets or from online spice purveyors. If you like, garnish the salad with edible flowers for color.

4 cups sugar snap peas (about 1 pound), trimmed

1 bunch radishes, trimmed

¼ cup torn fresh mint

½ cup soft sheep's-milk cheese, such as MitiCrema, *or* soft goat cheese

½ teaspoon salt

Ground pepper to taste

2 tablespoons lemon juice

2 tablespoons extra-virgin olive oil

Aleppo pepper for garnish

Edible flowers for garnish

Cut snap peas in half lengthwise. Very thinly slice radishes into coin shapes or half-moons. Toss the snap peas, radishes, mint and cheese in a large bowl. Season with salt and pepper, then toss with lemon juice and oil. Serve garnished with a sprinkle of Aleppo pepper and flowers, if desired.

SERVES 5: about 1 cup each

Calories 135 | **Fat** 9g (sat 3g) | **Cholesterol** 7mg | **Carbohydrates** 9g | **Total sugars** 4g (added 0g) | **Protein** 6g | **Fiber** 3g | **Sodium** 316mg | **Potassium** 294mg. **Nutrition bonus:** Vitamin C (104% daily value) | Vitamin A (26% dv).

Simple Swaps

• Fresh asparagus, snow peas, green beans or edamame can stand in for the snap peas.

• Use any soft herbs, such as basil, tarragon or even chives.

• Consider swapping a crumbly goat's-milk feta or a blue cheese like Maytag for the soft sheep's-milk cheese.

pineapple & avocado salad

This refreshing Cuban-style salad captures the flavors of the tropics. The green and gold hues are especially welcome in late winter, when California avocados and Hawaiian pineapples are in season. Serve alongside grilled chicken or pork, with steamed brown rice and black beans.

1/4 **cup thinly sliced red onion, separated into rings**
   Ice water

1 **medium fresh pineapple**

3 **tablespoons extra-virgin olive oil**

1 **tablespoon fresh lime juice**

2 **firm ripe avocados, sliced**

1/2 **teaspoon kosher salt**
   Ground pepper to taste (optional)

1. Soak onion in a small bowl of ice water for 15 minutes to mellow the bite.

2. Meanwhile, peel pineapple, halve lengthwise into quarters, remove the core and cut each quarter crosswise into slices.

3. Whisk oil and lime juice in a small bowl. Drain the onion and pat dry. Arrange half the avocado, pineapple and onion on a serving plate, sprinkle with 1/4 teaspoon salt and drizzle with half the dressing; repeat the layers. Garnish with pepper, if desired.

SERVES 8: 1 cup each

Calories 186 | Fat 13g (sat 2g) | Cholesterol 0mg | Carbohydrates 20g | Total sugars 12g (added 0g) | Protein 2g | Fiber 5g | Sodium 75mg | Potassium 374mg. Nutrition bonus: Vitamin C (100% daily value).

Simple Swaps

- Pineapple isn't the only fruit to give this simple salad its tropical flavor—mango and papaya are also good choices.

- If heat's your thing, add a pinch of Aleppo pepper, cayenne pepper, ground chipotle or crushed red pepper.

- Slice up a ripe tomato if you have one on hand and add it to the salad.

greek potato salad

This lightened potato salad features cherry tomatoes, olives, feta and a Dijon-shallot vinaigrette. Waxy potatoes, such as red and yellow, make the best salad because they hold their shape when cooked. Keep the potato skins on for more fiber and potassium. *(Photo: page 160.)*

$2^{1}/_{2}$ **pounds yellow *or* red potatoes, scrubbed and diced ($^{1}/_{2}$- to 1-inch)**

$^{3}/_{4}$ **teaspoon salt, divided**

$^{1}/_{4}$ **cup extra-virgin olive oil**

3 **tablespoons white-wine vinegar**

$^{1}/_{4}$ **cup finely chopped shallot**

1 **tablespoon Dijon mustard**

$^{1}/_{2}$ **teaspoon ground pepper**

1 **cup halved cherry tomatoes**

$^{1}/_{3}$ **cup crumbled feta cheese**

$^{1}/_{4}$ **cup quartered Kalamata olives**

2 **tablespoons chopped fresh oregano *or* 2 teaspoons dried**

1. Bring 1 inch of water to a boil in a large saucepan fitted with a steamer basket. Add potatoes, cover and cook until tender, 12 to 15 minutes. Spread in a single layer on a rimmed baking sheet and sprinkle with $^{1}/_{4}$ teaspoon salt; let cool 15 minutes.

2. Meanwhile, whisk oil, vinegar, shallot, mustard, pepper and the remaining $^{1}/_{2}$ teaspoon salt in a large bowl. Add the potatoes, tomatoes, feta, olives and oregano; stir well to coat. Serve at room temperature or refrigerate until cold.

SERVES 10: about $^{3}/_{4}$ cup each

Calories 170 | **Fat** 8g (sat 2g) | **Cholesterol** 4mg | **Carbohydrates** 22g | **Total sugars** 1g (added 0g) | **Protein** 3g | **Fiber** 2g | **Sodium** 308mg | **Potassium** 530mg.

Simple Swaps

• Roast the potatoes instead of steaming and, if you like, swap in a different variety like purple potatoes or even sweet potatoes.

• Make it creamy and swap $^{1}/_{2}$ cup each mayo and low-fat plain yogurt for the oil and vinegar.

• Load in the vegetables and fruits of your choice, such as green beans, snap peas, diced apple or even pickles.

roasting vegetables

Roasting vegetables is a quick way to give them a lot of flavor with very little work. **To roast vegetables:** Preheat oven to 450°F. Prepare vegetables of your choice. Toss with 4 teaspoons olive oil or canola oil, ¹/₂ teaspoon salt and ¹/₄ teaspoon pepper—or with one of the flavor combinations on page 177. Spread on a large rimmed baking sheet and roast until desired tenderness. Serves 4. (See below for prep instructions and timing.)

BEETS & TURNIPS

1¹/₂ pounds without greens, ends trimmed, peeled, cut into 1-inch pieces or wedges | 20 to 25 minutes

Beets: 116 calories | 16 g carbohydrates | 5 g fiber.
Turnips: 90 calories | 11 g carbohydrates | 3 g fiber.

BROCCOLI & CAULIFLOWER

1 pound, cut into 1-inch florets | 15 to 20 minutes

Broccoli: 74 calories | 6 g carbohydrates | 3 g fiber.
Cauliflower: 71 calories | 6 g carbohydrates | 2 g fiber.

BRUSSELS SPROUTS

1 pound, outer leaves removed, stems trimmed; larger ones quartered, smaller ones halved | 15 to 20 minutes

91 calories | 10 g carbohydrates | 4 g fiber.

CABBAGE

1¹/₂ pounds (1 small head), cored, cut into 1-inch squares | 15 to 20 minutes

75 calories | 7 g carbohydrates | 3 g fiber.

CARROTS & PARSNIPS

1¹/₂ pounds, peeled or scrubbed, woody core removed from parsnips; cut into ¹/₄-inch slices | 20 to 25 minutes

Carrots: 104 calories | 15 g carbohydrates | 4 g fiber.
Parsnips: 137 calories | 23 g carbohydrates | 5 g fiber.

FENNEL

2 large bulbs, stalks and fronds removed, bulb cored and cut into 1-inch wedges | 25 to 30 minutes

79 calories | 9 g carbohydrates | 4 g fiber.

GREEN BEANS

1 pound, stem ends trimmed | 15 to 20 minutes

78 calories | 8 g carbohydrates | 3 g fiber.

POTATOES & SWEET POTATOES

1¹/₂ pounds, scrubbed (peeled if desired), cut into 1-inch pieces or wedges | 20 to 25 minutes

Potatoes: 182 calories | 30 g carbohydrates | 2 g fiber.
Sweet Potatoes: 195 calories | 35 g carbohydrates | 6 g fiber.

SUMMER SQUASH & ZUCCHINI

1 pound, quartered lengthwise, cut into 1-inch pieces | 15 to 20 minutes

62 calories | 4 g carbohydrates | 1 g fiber.

*Nutritional analysis per serving based on vegetables prepared with oil, as specified above.

grilling vegetables

Cooking vegetables on the grill imparts a delicious smokiness. So if the grill's already on for dinner, why not put some vegetables on too? **To grill vegetables:** Preheat grill to medium-high. Prepare vegetables of your choice. Brush with 1 tablespoon olive oil or canola oil and sprinkle with $1/4$ teaspoon each salt and pepper—or with one of the flavor combinations on page 177. Grill, turning occasionally, until lightly charred and tender. Serves 4. (See below for prep instructions and timing.)

ASPARAGUS

1 pound, trimmed | 6 to 8 minutes

55 calories | 4 g carbohydrates | 2 g fiber.

BELL PEPPERS

2 large peppers, halved, seeded and stemmed | 5 minutes

57 calories | 6 g carbohydrates | 1 g fiber.

CORN

4 ears, husked | 8 to 12 minutes

119 calories | 19 g carbohydrates | 2 g fiber.

EGGPLANT

1 pound, cut into $1/4$-inch-thick rounds | 2 to 3 minutes

60 calories | 7 g carbohydrates | 4 g fiber.

MUSHROOMS, PORTOBELLO

4 large, stems removed; scrape out gills with a spoon | 6 to 8 minutes

49 calories | 3 g carbohydrates | 1 g fiber.

ONIONS

2 medium, peeled and cut into $1/4$-inch-thick rounds | 2 to 3 minutes

54 calories | 5 g carbohydrates | 1 g fiber.

SUMMER SQUASH & ZUCCHINI

1 pound, sliced diagonally $1/4$ inch thick | 4 to 6 minutes

49 calories | 4 g carbohydrates | 1 g fiber.

*Nutritional analysis per serving based on vegetables prepared with oil, as specified above.

sautéing vegetables

Sautéing is an easy way to cook vegetables in a flash. **To sauté vegetables:** Prepare vegetables of your choice. Heat 1 tablespoon olive oil or canola oil or butter in a large skillet over medium heat. Add the vegetables and cook, stirring frequently, until tender. Serves 4. (See below for prep instructions and timing.) Season with one of our favorite flavor combinations on page 177, if desired.

ASPARAGUS

1 pound, trimmed and cut into 1-inch pieces | 5 to 7 minutes

55 calories | 4 g carbohydrates | 2 g fiber.

CARROTS

1 pound, cut into $1/8$-inch rounds | 4 to 6 minutes

78 calories | 11 g carbohydrates | 3 g fiber.

CHARD, COLLARD GREENS & KALE

$1^1/4$ pounds, trimmed and leaves chopped | 4 to 6 minutes

Chard: 57 calories | 5 g carbohydrates | 3 g fiber.

Collard greens: 86 calories | 9 g carbohydrates | 7 g fiber.

Kale: 74 calories | 8 g carbohydrates | 3 g fiber.

CORN

4 ears, remove kernels from cobs | 3 to 5 minutes

119 calories | 19 g carbohydrates | 2 g fiber.

GREEN BEANS

1 pound, stem ends trimmed | 8 to 10 minutes

70 calories | 9 g carbohydrates | 4 g fiber.

PEAS, SNAP OR SNOW

1 pound, trimmed | 2 to 3 minutes

79 calories | 9 g carbohydrates | 3 g fiber.

SPINACH

$1^1/4$ pounds, trimmed, tough stems removed | 2 to 4 minutes

57 calories | 4 g carbohydrates | 3 g fiber.

SUMMER SQUASH & ZUCCHINI

1 pound, $1/4$-inch slices | 6 to 8 minutes

51 calories | 4 g carbohydrates | 1 g fiber.

WINTER SQUASH, DELICATA

1 large, halved lengthwise, seeded, thinly sliced | 10 minutes

83 calories | 13 g carbohydrates | 2 g fiber.

---

*Nutritional analysis per serving based on vegetables prepared with oil, as specified above.

steaming vegetables

Steamed vegetables can't be beat for simplicity or healthfulness. Serve them plain or with a drizzle of olive oil and a little salt and pepper—or season them with one of the flavor combinations opposite. **To steam vegetables:** Prepare vegetables of your choice. Bring 1 inch of water to a boil in a large saucepan fitted with a steamer basket. Add the vegetables, cover and steam until just tender. Serves 4. (See below for prep instructions and timing.)

ASPARAGUS

$1\frac{1}{2}$ pounds (1 or 2 bunches), trimmed | 4 minutes

35 calories | 7 g carbohydrates | 3 g fiber.

BEETS

$1\frac{1}{2}$ pounds without greens, ends trimmed, peeled, cut into 1-inch pieces or wedges | 10 to 15 minutes

49 calories | 11 g carbohydrates | 3 g fiber.

BROCCOLI & CAULIFLOWER

1 pound broccoli, $1\frac{1}{2}$ to 2 pounds cauliflower (about 1 head), cut into 1-inch florets | 5 to 6 minutes

Broccoli: 40 calories | 8 g carbohydrates | 4 g fiber.
Cauliflower: 38 calories | 7 g carbohydrates | 4 g fiber.

BRUSSELS SPROUTS

1 pound, stems trimmed | 6 to 8 minutes

45 calories | 9 g carbohydrates | 3 g fiber.

CARROTS

$1\frac{1}{2}$ pounds, cut into $\frac{1}{8}$-inch slices | 4 minutes

62 calories | 15 g carbohydrates | 4 g fiber.

GREEN BEANS

1 pound, stem ends trimmed | 5 minutes

39 calories | 9 g carbohydrates | 4 g fiber.

PEAS, SNAP OR SNOW

1 pound, trimmed | 3 to 5 minutes

48 calories | 9 g carbohydrates | 3 g fiber.

POTATOES (BABY), RED OR YUKON GOLD

$1\frac{1}{2}$ pounds, scrubbed | 10 to 15 minutes

119 calories | 27 g carbohydrates | 3 g fiber.

*Nutritional analysis per serving based on plain vegetables, prepared as specified above.

seasoning suggestions for cooked vegetables

To top grilled or roasted vegetables

CHILE-GARLIC & SOY

Before grilling or roasting: Toss the vegetables with 4 teaspoons olive oil or canola oil, 1 tablespoon each chile-garlic sauce and reduced-sodium soy sauce and $1/8$ teaspoon ground white pepper.

CHILI-LIME

Before grilling or roasting: Toss the vegetables with 4 teaspoons canola oil, $3/4$ teaspoon each chili powder and ground cumin and $1/2$ teaspoon salt.

After grilling or roasting: Toss with 2 tablespoons chopped fresh cilantro and lime juice to taste.

GARLIC-THYME

Before grilling or roasting: Toss the vegetables with 2 tablespoons olive oil, 1 tablespoon chopped fresh thyme (or 1 teaspoon dried), $1/2$ teaspoon garlic powder and $1/4$ teaspoon each salt and pepper.

After grilling or roasting: Toss with 2 tablespoons chopped fennel fronds, if desired.

SPICY ORANGE

Before grilling or roasting: Toss the vegetables with 4 teaspoons olive oil, the zest of 1 orange, $1/2$ teaspoon salt and $1/4$ to $1/2$ teaspoon crushed red pepper.

To toss with sautéed vegetables

CAPER & PARSLEY

Combine $1/3$ cup chopped shallot, $1/4$ cup flat-leaf parsley leaves, 3 tablespoons rinsed capers, 2 tablespoons white-wine vinegar and $1/4$ teaspoon each salt and pepper.

MUSTARD-SCALLION

Combine $1/4$ cup sliced scallions, 2 tablespoons Dijon mustard, 1 tablespoon lemon juice and $1/4$ teaspoon each salt and pepper.

SESAME-ORANGE

Combine 3 tablespoons orange juice, 1 teaspoon sesame oil and $1/4$ teaspoon each salt and pepper. Sprinkle with 2 teaspoons toasted sesame seeds (*see Tip, page 247*).

To top or toss with steamed vegetables

CREAMY GARLIC

Mash 1 minced small garlic clove with $1/2$ teaspoon kosher salt. Whisk with $1/2$ cup plain yogurt, 1 tablespoon each olive oil and chopped fresh parsley, and pepper to taste.

FRESH TOMATO & SHALLOT

Combine 2 chopped tomatoes, 1 minced shallot, 1 tablespoon each olive oil and balsamic vinegar and $1/4$ teaspoon each salt and pepper.

LEMON-DILL

Whisk 4 teaspoons chopped fresh dill, 1 tablespoon each minced shallot, olive oil and lemon juice, 1 teaspoon whole-grain mustard and $1/4$ teaspoon each salt and pepper.

grain-cooking guide

Here's an easy guide to cooking healthy grains. Start with 1 cup of uncooked grain; a serving size is $1/2$ cup of cooked grain. (See below for prep instructions and timing.) Serve plain or season with one of our whole-grain flavoring combinations opposite, if desired.

BARLEY (PEARL)

1 cup barley and $2^1/2$ cups water or broth
Bring barley and liquid to a boil. Reduce heat to low, cover and simmer for 35 to 50 minutes.
YIELD: $3-3^1/2$ cups
PER SERVING: 297 calories | 22 g carbohydrates | 3 g fiber.

BULGUR

1 cup bulgur and $1^1/2$ cups water or broth
Bring bulgur and liquid to a boil. Reduce heat to low, cover and simmer until tender and most of the liquid has been absorbed, 10 to 15 minutes.
YIELD: $2^1/2-3$ cups
PER SERVING: 76 calories | 17 g carbohydrates | 4 g fiber.

COUSCOUS (WHOLE-WHEAT)

1 cup couscous and $1^3/4$ cups water or broth
Bring liquid to a boil; stir in couscous. Remove from heat, cover and let stand for 5 minutes. Fluff with a fork.
YIELD: $3-3^1/2$ cups
PER SERVING: 113 calories | 25 g carbohydrates | 4 g fiber.

POLENTA (CORNMEAL)

1 cup polenta and $4^1/3$ cups water or broth
Bring cold water and 1 teaspoon salt (or broth) to a boil. Slowly whisk in cornmeal until smooth. Reduce heat to low, cover and simmer, stirring occasionally, until very thick and creamy, 10 to 15 minutes.
YIELD: $4-4^1/3$ cups
PER SERVING: 55 calories | 12 g carbohydrates | 1 g fiber.

QUINOA

1 cup quinoa and 2 cups water or broth
Bring quinoa and liquid to a boil. Reduce heat to low, cover and simmer until tender and most of the liquid has been absorbed, 15 to 20 minutes. Fluff with a fork.
YIELD: 3 cups
PER SERVING: 111 calories | 20 g carbohydrates | 3 g fiber.

RICE, BROWN

1 cup brown rice and $2^1/2$ cups water or broth
Bring rice and liquid to a boil. Reduce heat to low, cover and simmer until tender and most of the liquid has been absorbed, 40 to 50 minutes. Let stand for 5 minutes. Fluff with a fork.
YIELD: 3 cups
PER SERVING: 109 calories | 23 g carbohydrates | 2 g fiber.

RICE, WILD

1 cup wild rice and at least 4 cups water or broth
Cook rice in a large saucepan of lightly salted boiling water (or broth) until tender, 45 to 55 minutes. Drain.
YIELD: $2-2^1/2$ cups
PER SERVING: 83 calories | 18 g carbohydrates | 1 g fiber.

In a hurry? Make instant brown rice, quick-cooking barley or quick-cooking wild rice, ready in 10 minutes or less (follow package directions).

---

*Nutritional analysis per $1/2$-cup serving based on grain prepared with water, as specified above.

flavoring suggestions for cooked whole grains

APRICOT NUT

Stir in $1/3$ cup chopped dried apricots, $1/4$ cup chopped toasted nuts (such as walnuts, pecans or pistachios; *see Tip, page 247*), 3 tablespoons orange juice, 1 teaspoon olive oil, and salt & pepper to taste.

LIME-CILANTRO

Stir in $2/3$ cup coarsely chopped fresh cilantro, $1/3$ cup chopped scallions, 2 tablespoons lime juice, and salt & pepper to taste.

MEDITERRANEAN

Stir in 1 chopped medium tomato, $1/4$ cup chopped Kalamata olives, $1/2$ teaspoon herbes de Provence, and salt & pepper to taste.

MINT & FETA

Stir in $3/4$ cup sliced scallions, $1/4$ cup each finely crumbled feta cheese and sliced fresh mint, and salt & pepper to taste.

PARMESAN & BALSAMIC

Stir in $1/4$ cup freshly grated Parmesan cheese, 1 teaspoon butter, 2 teaspoons balsamic vinegar, and salt & pepper to taste.

PARMESAN-DILL

Stir in $1/3$ cup freshly grated Parmesan cheese, 2 tablespoons chopped fresh dill, 1 teaspoon lemon zest, and salt & pepper to taste.

PEAS & LEMON

Stir in 1 cup frozen peas; cover and let stand for 5 minutes. Stir in 3 tablespoons chopped fresh parsley, $1^1/2$ teaspoons olive oil, 1 teaspoon lemon zest, and salt & pepper to taste.

SPINACH

Stir in 3 cups sliced baby spinach (or arugula); cover and let stand for 5 minutes. Season with salt & pepper to taste.

TOMATO-TARRAGON

Stir in $3/4$ cup chopped tomatoes, 3 tablespoons minced fresh tarragon (or parsley or thyme), and salt & pepper to taste.

breakfasts
without the junk

Breakfast is one meal that often gets short shrift, but it shouldn't. That first meal kick-starts your metabolism, nourishes your body and brain, and gives you energy to make it through the day. But it's also full of potential pitfalls—store-bought options can be junked-out with loads of sugar and refined grains. Then there's plenty of fast food or the pastry case at the coffee shop waiting to sabotage you. A clean quick breakfast can be as simple as a piece of whole-grain toast with peanut butter or a bowl of plain yogurt with fruit. But if you're looking for more stepped-up ideas, the recipes in this chapter, from a vegetarian hash to a broccoli omelet, are just the ticket. Even when you've only got time for breakfast on the go, it's possible to make it healthy—Jason Mraz's green smoothie on page 190 is proof of that.

Tomatillo Breakfast Tacos *(page 193)*

ACTIVE | 25 min
TOTAL | 45 min

To Make Ahead: Prepare Steps 2 and 3, keeping onion mixture, dry and wet ingredients separate; refrigerate for up 1 day. Continue with Step 4 just before baking.

savory prosciutto muffins

Onions caramelized in butter give these muffins a sweet and savory flavor. The prosciutto adds a hit of salt and richness. Serrano ham or other cured ham can be used in place of the prosciutto; just watch that it isn't cured with sugar.

2 tablespoons unsalted butter

1¹/₂ cups finely chopped onion

¹/₂ cup minced prosciutto (2 ounces)

2 cups whole-wheat pastry flour

1 teaspoon minced fresh rosemary

1¹/₂ teaspoons baking powder

¹/₂ teaspoon baking soda

¹/₂ teaspoon salt

¹/₈ teaspoon ground pepper

1 cup buttermilk

2 large eggs

2 tablespoons extra-virgin olive oil

1. Preheat oven to 400°F. Coat 12 (¹/₂-cup) muffin cups with cooking spray.

2. Melt butter in a large skillet over medium heat. Add onion and cook, stirring, until golden, about 5 minutes. Stir in prosciutto and cook, stirring, for 2 minutes. Remove from the heat.

3. Whisk flour, rosemary, baking powder, baking soda, salt and pepper in a large bowl until combined. Whisk buttermilk, eggs and oil in a medium bowl until blended.

4. Fold the onion mixture and buttermilk mixture into the dry ingredients with a rubber spatula until evenly moistened. Divide the batter among the prepared muffin cups.

5. Bake the muffins until lightly browned and a toothpick inserted in the center comes out clean, 18 to 20 minutes. Serve warm.

MAKES: 1 dozen muffins

Calories 149 | Fat 6g (sat 2g) | Cholesterol 40mg | Carbohydrates 18g | Total sugars 2g (added 0g) | Protein 5g | Fiber 2g | Sodium 357mg | Potassium 47mg.

clean it up

Prosciutto delivers distinct sweet-savory taste along with saltiness, allowing it to make a major flavor impact even when you use it sparingly. It's traditionally cured using only salt, which means it won't deliver added sugars as some other cured meats like bacon can.

ACTIVE 40 min
TOTAL 40 min

To Make Ahead:
Steam potatoes (Step 1);
refrigerate for up to 2 days.

potato, asparagus & mushroom hash

Made with asparagus, roasted red peppers and mushrooms, this updated vegetarian hash has a fresh springtime taste. Serve it topped with a poached egg or two and hearty whole-grain toast or sliced fresh fruit.

1 **pound new** *or* **baby potatoes, scrubbed, halved if large**

3 **tablespoons extra-virgin olive oil, divided**

1 **bunch asparagus (about 1 pound), trimmed and cut into** 1/2-**inch pieces**

4 **ounces shiitake mushroom caps** *or* **other mushrooms, sliced**

1 **shallot, minced**

1 **clove garlic, minced**

1 **small onion, coarsely chopped**

1/2 **cup chopped jarred roasted red peppers, rinsed**

1 **tablespoon minced fresh sage**

1/2 **teaspoon salt**

1/4 **teaspoon ground pepper**

Fresh chives for garnish

1. Bring 1 inch of water to a boil in a large sauce-pan fitted with a steamer basket. Add potatoes, cover and steam until barely tender when pierced with a skewer, 12 to 15 minutes, depending on size. When cool enough to handle, chop into 1/2-inch pieces.

2. Heat 1 tablespoon oil in a large skillet over medium heat. Add asparagus, mushrooms, shallot and garlic and cook, stirring often, until beginning to brown, 5 to 7 minutes. Transfer to a plate.

3. Add the remaining 2 tablespoons oil to the pan. Add onion and the potatoes and cook, stirring occasionally and scraping up the browned bits with a metal spatula, until the potatoes are browned, 4 to 8 minutes. Return the asparagus mixture to the pan along with roasted peppers, sage, salt and pepper; cook, stirring, until heated through, about 1 minute more. Serve sprinkled with chives, if desired.

SERVES 4: about 1 1/4 cups each

Calories 239 | **Fat** 11g (sat 2g) | **Cholesterol** 0mg | **Carbohydrates** 29g | **Total sugars** 4g (added 0g) | **Protein** 5g | **Fiber** 4g | **Sodium** 492mg | **Potassium** 777mg. **Nutrition bonus:** Vitamin C (29% daily value) | Folate (28% dv) | Vitamin A (21% dv).

ACTIVE | 35 min
TOTAL | 1 hr 35 min

To Make Ahead:
Prepare through Step 2 and refrigerate for up to 1 day or individually wrap and freeze for up to 3 months; thaw overnight in the refrigerator before cooking.

pistachio breakfast sausage patties

Transform basic breakfast sausage into something special with only a few simple ingredients. Pistachios are a surprising addition and add a slightly sweet note. Plenty of black pepper, a big pinch of cayenne and minced garlic make the sausage pleasantly spicy—use less if you prefer. The recipe yields 8 small patties, but can easily be doubled and cooked in two batches.

- 2 teaspoons fennel seeds
- 8 ounces ground pork breakfast sausage (*see Tip*)
- 8 ounces ground turkey breast
- 2 cloves garlic, finely minced
- 1 teaspoon coarsely ground pepper
- 1/8 teaspoon cayenne pepper (optional)
- 1/2 cup coarsely chopped unsalted pistachios
- 1/2 cup finely minced flat-leaf parsley

1. Grind fennel seeds in a spice grinder or with a mortar and pestle until finely ground.

2. Place pork and turkey in a large bowl. Sprinkle with the fennel, garlic, pepper and cayenne (if using) and combine using your hands or a spoon. Add pistachios and parsley; mix just until evenly incorporated. With dampened hands, form eight 3-inch patties using a generous 1/4 cup each. Place on a baking sheet or large plate. Cover and refrigerate for at least 1 hour and up to 1 day.

3. When ready to cook, cover a large plate with paper towels and line a baking sheet with foil. Preheat oven to 300°F.

4. Cook patties in a large nonstick skillet over medium heat, turning once, until nicely brown on both sides and no longer pink in the middle, 5 to 9 minutes per side. Transfer to the prepared plate to drain briefly, then place on the prepared baking sheet and transfer to the oven to keep warm until ready to serve. (Don't keep in the oven for longer than 30 minutes, or they'll dry out.)

SERVES 8: 1 2-oz. patty each

Calories 132 | Fat 9g (sat 2g) | Cholesterol 24mg | Carbohydrates 4g | Total sugars 1g (added 0g) | Protein 10g | Fiber 1g | Sodium 198mg | Potassium 217mg.

 clean it up

Store-bought breakfast sausages often contain added sugars and loads of sodium. Opt for a brand that has no more than 500 mg of sodium per 2-ounce serving and 0 grams of sugar.

broccoli & parmesan cheese omelet

A high-protein veggie omelet is a terrific way to start your day off right. To switch it up, swap out the broccoli for spinach, kale or asparagus and follow the same method, adjusting cooking times as needed.

2 large eggs

2 large egg whites

1 teaspoon extra-virgin olive oil

¹⁄₂ cup chopped broccoli

1 shallot, finely chopped

¹⁄₄ cup finely grated Parmigiano-Reggiano cheese

1 slice sprouted-grain bread *(see Tip)*, **toasted**

1. Whisk eggs and egg whites in a small bowl; place near the stove.

2. Heat oil in a medium nonstick skillet over medium heat. Add broccoli and shallot; cook, stirring frequently, until tender, 3 to 5 minutes. Pour the eggs into the pan, reduce heat to medium-low and cook, stirring constantly with a heatproof rubber spatula, until the eggs are starting to set, about 10 seconds. Cover and cook for 1 minute. Sprinkle with cheese, reduce heat to low, cover and cook until set, about 3 minutes more. Serve with toast.

SERVES 1

Calories 407 | **Fat** 20g (sat 7g) | **Cholesterol** 386mg | **Carbohydrates** 22g | **Total sugars** 2g (added 0g) | **Protein** 33g | **Fiber** 4g | **Sodium** 603mg | **Potassium** 447mg. **Nutrition bonus:** Vitamin C (58% daily value) | Vitamin A (40% dv) | Calcium (34% dv) | Folate & Vitamin B$_{12}$ (21% dv).

clean it up

Though research has shown some health benefits from sprouted grains, including increased nutrient availability and lower glycemic response, breads made with them aren't automatically a healthier choice. Some sprouted-grain breads contain quite a bit of added sugars and salt. Look for varieties that have no added sweeteners in the ingredients and 200mg or less sodium per slice.

jason mraz's avocado green smoothie

Avocado adds richness and healthy fat, dark leafy greens add plenty of vitamins and minerals, and banana adds a touch of sweetness to this on-the-go breakfast. To make this even more of a meal-in-a-glass, singer-songwriter and avocado farmer Jason Mraz adds a tablespoon of coconut oil and some sprouted flax or chia seeds.

1¼ cups cold unsweetened almond milk *or* coconut milk beverage *(see Tip)*

1 ripe avocado, pitted and peeled

1 ripe banana

1 sweet apple, such as Honeycrisp, sliced

½ large *or* 1 small stalk celery, chopped

2 cups lightly packed kale leaves *or* spinach

1 1-inch piece peeled fresh ginger

8 ice cubes

Blend milk beverage, avocado, banana, apple, celery, kale (or spinach), ginger and ice in a blender until very smooth.

SERVES 2: 2 cups each

Calories 307 | **Fat** 17g (sat 2g) | **Cholesterol** 0mg | **Carbohydrates** 40g | **Total sugars** 18g (added 0g) | **Protein** 5g | **Fiber** 12g | **Sodium** 144mg | **Potassium** 1,095mg. **Nutrition bonus:** Vitamin C (66% daily value) | Vitamin A (44% dv) | Folate (31% dv).

clean it up

Most store-bought nondairy milks and beverages contain stabilizers and thickening agents, such as gums, lecithin and carrageenan, to provide a smooth mouthfeel and texture. You may want to choose one without carrageenan, a thickener made from seaweed, as some research shows it may cause digestive-system inflammation. Many widely available brands have reformulated their milks to remove carrageenan and replace it with gums (guar, gellan, locust bean, xanthan), which are all considered OK for most people by the Center for Science in the Public Interest (CSPI). However, if you have IBS or other intestinal sensitivities, be aware that even these stabilizers might cause increased symptoms and are best avoided.

avocado toast
with egg, cheddar & kimchi

For the most satisfying avocado-egg toast, go for full-flavored, high-fiber bread, like a hearty slice of German-style rye or seeded multigrain. To turn this into a portable breakfast, swap the toast for a whole-wheat English muffin. Look for jars of kimchi in the refrigerated section of well-stocked supermarkets or natural-foods stores.

$1/2$ **small avocado, mashed**

1 **slice whole-grain bread, toasted**

Pinch of ground pepper

2 **tablespoons shredded Cheddar cheese**

$1/2$ **teaspoon extra-virgin olive oil**

1 **large egg**

2 **tablespoons coarsely chopped kimchi**

1. Spread avocado on toast; season with pepper and sprinkle with cheese. Heat in a toaster oven (or broil) until the cheese melts.

2. Meanwhile, heat oil in a small nonstick skillet over medium heat. Crack egg into the pan. Reduce heat to medium-low and cook 5 to 7 minutes for a soft-set yolk. Top the toast with the egg and kimchi.

SERVES 1

Calories 417 | Fat 27g (sat 7g) | Cholesterol 200mg | Carbohydrates 29g | Total sugars 1g (added 0g) | Protein 15g | Fiber 8g | Sodium 460mg | Potassium 569mg. **Nutrition bonus:** Folate (27% daily value).

tomatillo breakfast tacos

These tasty breakfast tacos are a satisfying way to start the day. *Queso blanco*, also known as *queso fresco*, is a soft, slightly salty fresh Mexican cheese. Look for it in Latin markets and well-stocked supermarkets. *(Photo: page 180.)*

1 tablespoon extra-virgin olive oil

6 medium tomatillos (about 8 ounces), husked, rinsed and coarsely chopped

¼ cup chopped onion

2 cloves garlic, minced

4 large eggs, lightly beaten

¼ teaspoon ground pepper

⅛ teaspoon salt

4 small (4- to 5-inch) corn *or* whole-wheat tortillas *(see Tip)*, warmed

¼ cup crumbled queso blanco *or* feta cheese

Heat oil in a large nonstick skillet over medium heat. Add tomatillos, onion and garlic and cook, stirring, until most of the liquid from the tomatillos has evaporated, 8 to 12 minutes. Add eggs, pepper and salt and cook, stirring, until the eggs are just set, 2 to 3 minutes more. Divide the scrambled eggs among the tortillas and sprinkle with cheese.

SERVES 2: 2 tacos each

Calories 418 | Fat 24g (sat 8g) | Cholesterol 389mg | Carbohydrates 32g | Total sugars 6g (added 0g) | Protein 20g | Fiber 5g | Sodium 498mg | Potassium 560mg. Nutrition bonus: Vitamin C (24% daily value) | Calcium (23% dv).

 *clean it up*

Opting for a flour tortilla? Check that the first ingredient on the label is "whole-wheat" flour or "whole-grain" flour and that it doesn't contain any partially hydrogenated oil. Corn tortillas are made from masa, a type of flour made from soaking corn in a lime solution, which adds calcium and makes B vitamins and protein more available, while only losing a little of the bran. Some brands contain added sugars, such as corn syrup; check the ingredients label and skip those that do.

clean on the go:
lunches
& snacks

If you're busy juggling activities, work or social commitments during the day, that can often mean grabbing lunch or a snack while you're out and about. And while there are good options to be found (think: a bag of nuts at the gas station or a salad at a supermarket), this could also mean feeding dollars into the vending machine or grabbing questionable prepared meals from the store. But with a little forethought you can have homemade clean lunches and snacks to tote along wherever you go. Keeping a container of homemade trail mix, mango-date energy bites or lemony popcorn at the ready will help squelch sneaky snack attacks. And, an array of make-ahead soups, from tomato to Mediterranean lentil, provide quick ways to get a midday energy boost.

Bean & Barley Soup (page 201)

To Make Ahead:
Refrigerate for up to
4 days or freeze for up
to 3 months.

quick tomato soup

This is a great "pantry soup"—that is, it comes together in minutes from ingredients that you can keep on hand all the time—and it's far tastier than canned soup. A mixture of chicken broth and half-and-half keeps it healthy yet still decadent-tasting.

1 tablespoon butter

1 tablespoon extra-virgin olive oil

1 medium onion, chopped

1 stalk celery, chopped

2 cloves garlic, chopped

1 teaspoon chopped fresh thyme *or* **parsley**

1 28-ounce can whole peeled tomatoes

1 14-ounce can whole peeled tomatoes

4 cups reduced-sodium chicken broth, "no-chicken" broth *or* **vegetable broth**

½ cup half-and-half (optional)

½ teaspoon salt

Ground pepper to taste

1. Heat butter and oil in a large pot over medium heat until the butter has melted. Add onion and celery; cook, stirring occasionally, until softened, 4 to 6 minutes. Add garlic and thyme (or parsley); cook, stirring, until fragrant, about 10 seconds.

2. Stir in canned tomatoes (with juice). Add broth; bring to a lively simmer over high heat. Reduce heat to maintain a lively simmer and cook for 10 minutes.

3. Puree the soup in the pot using an immersion blender or in batches in a blender. (Use caution when pureeing hot liquids.) Stir in half-and-half (if using), salt and pepper.

SERVES 4: about 2 cups each

Calories 158 | **Fat** 9g (sat 3g) | **Cholesterol** 8mg | **Carbohydrates** 17g | **Total sugars** 8g (added 0g) | **Protein** 8g | **Fiber** 5g | **Sodium** 715mg | **Potassium** 851mg. **Nutrition bonus:** Vitamin C (68% daily value) | Vitamin A (27% dv).

chilly dilly cucumber soup

ACTIVE 50 min

TOTAL **3 hrs 50 min**
(including 3 hrs
chilling time)

To Make Ahead:
Prepare through Step 4
and refrigerate for up to
3 days.

This cold soup has a surprisingly seductive taste. The secret is that both the broth and the yogurt garnish are loaded with fresh dill and chives. The recipe calls for "handfuls" of herbs; if you are relying on the grocery store instead of the garden or farmers' market, you'll need about one large bunch or a couple of 2- to 3-ounce packets.

4 cups reduced-sodium chicken broth *(see Tip, page 200)*

1½ cups chopped peeled waxy, thin-skinned potatoes (such as red *or* Yukon Gold, not russets)

½ cup chopped cauliflower *or* ½ cup additional chopped peeled potato

½ cup chopped celery

1 large handful whole fresh dill sprigs (including stems) plus ¼ cup coarsely chopped dill leaves, divided, plus small sprigs for garnish

1 handful whole fresh chives plus ¼ cup coarsely chopped chives, divided, plus more for garnish

1 cup low-fat *or* nonfat plain yogurt

1 tablespoon butter

1¼ cups finely diced seeded peeled cucumber, plus thin half-moon slices for garnish

Ground pepper to taste

1. Combine broth, potatoes, cauliflower (or additional potato) and celery in a large saucepan. Lay dill sprigs and whole chives on top. Bring to a boil over medium-high heat. Adjust the heat so it boils briskly and cook until the vegetables are very tender when pierced with a fork, 15 to 18 minutes. Remove from the heat and set aside until cooled slightly.

2. Meanwhile, combine chopped dill and chopped chives with yogurt in a food processor. Process until the herbs are finely chopped and the mixture is slightly green. Transfer half the mixture to a bowl; cover and refrigerate to use later as a garnish. Leave the remainder in the processor.

3. Using a fork, lift off and discard the herbs from the pan. Transfer the vegetables to the processor with a slotted spoon (leave the broth in the pan). Add butter; process until very smooth, scraping down the sides as needed.

continued

4. Add diced cucumber to the broth. Bring to a gentle boil and cook until the cucumber is just cooked through but still slightly crisp, about 3 minutes. Remove from heat. Thoroughly stir the pureed vegetables into the cucumber mixture. Season with pepper. Refrigerate until chilled, at least 3 hours or up to 3 days.

5. Serve the soup with a dollop of the reserved herbed yogurt. Garnish with small sprigs of dill, chopped chives and/or half-moons of cucumber, if desired.

SERVES 5: about 1 cup each

Calories 106 | Fat 3g (sat 2g) | Cholesterol 9mg | Carbohydrates 14g | Total sugars 5g (added 0g) | Protein 6g | Fiber 1g | Sodium 491mg | Potassium 503mg.

 clean it up

Homemade broth or stock is cleanest, but store-bought broth is a convenient option. Choose one with no added sugar (many brands contain small amounts of it in the form of dextrose) and with less than 200 mg of sodium per cup (there's a lot of added sodium in some brands). You may also find "natural flavors" in the ingredients. The FDA considers them safe, but since the ingredients label often doesn't tell you what the source of the flavoring is, it could be from an animal or insect that sounds less than appealing.

bean & barley soup

ACTIVE 30 min
TOTAL 45 min

To Make Ahead:
Refrigerate for up to
3 days or freeze for
up to 6 months.

This hearty soup tastes like it has simmered for hours, but actually it's quite quick to put together. Plus, it freezes beautifully. If you have cooked barley on hand, omit the quick barley and stir in 1 1/2 cups cooked barley along with the spinach in Step 2. *(Photo: page 194.)*

4 teaspoons extra-virgin olive oil

1 large onion, chopped

1 medium fennel bulb, cored and chopped

5 cloves garlic, minced

1 teaspoon dried basil

1 15-ounce can cannellini *or* other white beans, rinsed

1 14-ounce can fire-roasted diced tomatoes

6 cups low-sodium vegetable broth

3/4 cup quick barley

1 5-ounce package baby spinach (6 cups)

1/4 cup grated Parmesan cheese

1/4 teaspoon ground pepper

1. Heat oil in a large pot over medium-high heat. Add onion, fennel, garlic and basil; cook, stirring frequently, until the vegetables are tender and just beginning to brown, 6 to 8 minutes.

2. Mash 1/2 cup of beans. Stir the mashed and whole beans, tomatoes, broth and barley into the pot. Bring to a boil over high heat. Reduce heat to medium and simmer, stirring occasionally, until the barley is tender, about 15 minutes. Stir in spinach and cook until wilted, about 1 minute. Remove from heat and stir in cheese and pepper.

SERVES 4: 2 1/2 cups each

Calories 323 | Fat 7g (sat 2g) | Cholesterol 4mg | Carbohydrates 57g | Total sugars 11g (added 0g) | Protein 15g | Fiber 13g | Sodium 804mg | Potassium 1,060mg. Nutrition bonus: Vitamin A (108% daily value) | Vitamin C (66% dv) | Folate (48% dv) | Iron (21% dv) | Calcium (20% dv).

To Make Ahead: Prepare through Step 2 and refrigerate for up to 3 days or freeze for up to 6 months; stir in cilantro and lemon juice just before serving.

moroccan lentil soup

Like most soups, this flavorful Moroccan-spiced lentil soup gets better with time, so make it a day ahead if you can. To make it in a slow cooker, combine everything but the spinach, cilantro and lemon juice in a 5- to 6-quart slow cooker. Cover and cook until the lentils are tender, 4 to 5 hours on High or 8 to 10 hours on Low. During the last 30 minutes of cooking, stir in spinach. Just before serving, stir in cilantro and lemon juice.

2 teaspoons extra-virgin olive oil

2 cups chopped onions

2 cups chopped carrots

4 cloves garlic, minced

1 teaspoon ground coriander

1 teaspoon ground cumin

1 teaspoon ground turmeric

¹/₄ teaspoon ground cinnamon

¹/₄ teaspoon ground pepper

6 cups vegetable broth *or* reduced-sodium chicken broth

2 cups water

3 cups chopped cauliflower (about ¹/₂ medium)

1³/₄ cups green *or* brown lentils

1 28-ounce can diced tomatoes

2 tablespoons tomato paste

4 cups chopped fresh spinach *or* one 10-ounce package frozen chopped spinach, thawed

¹/₂ cup chopped fresh cilantro

2 tablespoons lemon juice

1. Heat oil in a large pot over medium heat; add onions and carrots and cook, stirring occasionally, until softened, about 10 minutes. Stir in garlic and cook for 30 seconds. Add coriander, cumin, turmeric, cinnamon and pepper; cook, stirring, until fragrant, about 1 minute.

2. Add broth, water, cauliflower, lentils, tomatoes and tomato paste; bring to a boil. Reduce heat and simmer, partially covered, stirring occasionally, until the lentils are tender but not mushy, 45 to 55 minutes. Stir in spinach and cook until wilted, about 5 minutes.

3. Just before serving, stir in cilantro and lemon juice.

SERVES 12: about 1¹/₄ cups each

Calories 151 | **Fat** 2g (sat 0g) | **Cholesterol** 0mg | **Carbohydrates** 27g | **Total sugars** 7g (added 0g) | **Protein** 9g | **Fiber** 9g | **Sodium** 599mg | **Potassium** 684mg. **Nutrition bonus:** Vitamin A (100% daily value) | Folate (47% dv) | Vitamin C (46% dv) | Iron (21% dv).

stuffed avocados

Forget the bread; next time you're serving seafood (or chicken or egg) salad for lunch, try mounding it in an avocado half instead.

1/4 **cup nonfat plain yogurt**

2 **tablespoons mayonnaise**

2 **tablespoons pimientos, rinsed and patted dry**

1 **small clove garlic, minced**

1/8 **teaspoon cayenne pepper, or to taste**

1/8 **teaspoon salt**

2²/₃ **cups cooked crabmeat** (*see Tip*), **picked over**

2 **ripe avocados, halved**

Lemon wedges for garnish

1. Combine yogurt, mayonnaise, pimientos, garlic, cayenne and salt in a blender. Blend until smooth. Transfer to a bowl and mix in crab.

2. Divide the crab salad among avocado halves. Serve with lemon wedges.

SERVES 4:1 stuffed avocado half each

Calories 236 | **Fat** 18g (sat 3g) | **Cholesterol** 34mg | **Carbohydrates** 10g | **Total sugars** 1g (added 0g) | **Protein** 12g | **Fiber** 7g | **Sodium** 230mg | **Potassium** 688mg. **Nutrition bonus:** Vitamin B_{12} (75% daily value) | Folate (25% dv) | Vitamin C (24% dv).

clean it up

Crab is delicious and lower in mercury than many types of seafood. King and snow crab from Alaska are currently the most sustainable, making Seafood Watch's "Best Choices" list, while blue and Dungeness crabs from the U.S. may be caught in a way that presents environmental concerns, and therefore make the "Good Alternative" list. Be wary of crab imported from Russia and Southeast Asia, which is currently on the guide's "Avoid" list due to overfishing. For more information, visit *seafoodwatch.org*.

beet & shrimp winter salad

This salad gets its staying power from protein-packed shrimp and fiber-rich barley. Look for precooked beets alongside other prepared vegetables in the produce department. To make zucchini ribbons, thinly shave whole zucchini lengthwise using a vegetable peeler. This recipe makes one hearty serving but can easily be expanded as needed. If you're taking this salad on the go for lunch, pack the dressing separately.

SALAD

- **2 cups lightly packed arugula**
- **1 cup lightly packed watercress**
- **1 cup cooked beet wedges**
- **1/2 cup zucchini ribbons**
- **1/2 cup thinly sliced fennel, fronds reserved for garnish**
- **1/2 cup cooked barley**
- **4 ounces peeled cooked shrimp, tails left on if desired**

VINAIGRETTE

- **2 tablespoons extra-virgin olive oil**
- **1 tablespoon red- or white-wine vinegar**
- **1/2 teaspoon Dijon mustard**
- **1/2 teaspoon minced shallot**
- **1/4 teaspoon ground pepper**
- **1/8 teaspoon salt**

1. **To prepare salad:** Arrange arugula, watercress, beets, zucchini, fennel, barley and shrimp on a large dinner plate.

2. **To prepare vinaigrette:** Whisk oil, vinegar, mustard, shallot, pepper and salt in a small bowl, then drizzle over the salad. Garnish with fennel fronds, if desired.

SERVES 1: about 4 1/2 cups

Calories 584 | Fat 30g (sat 4g) | Cholesterol 214mg | Carbohydrates 47g | Total sugars 18g (added 0g) | Protein 35g | Fiber 9g | Sodium 654mg | Potassium 1,506mg. Nutrition bonus: Vitamin C (72% daily value) | Folate (54% dv) | Vitamin A (53% dv) | Calcium (26% dv) | Iron (24% dv).

mediterranean tuna-spinach salad

Upgrade your tuna salad with black olives, feta and a tahini-lemon dressing. Served over baby spinach, this is an easy light lunch.

1½ **tablespoons tahini**

1½ **tablespoons lemon juice**

1½ **tablespoons water**

1 **5-ounce can chunk light tuna in water *(see Tip)*, drained**

4 **Kalamata olives, pitted and chopped**

2 **tablespoons feta cheese**

2 **tablespoons chopped fresh parsley**

2 **cups baby spinach**

Whisk tahini, lemon juice and water in a bowl. Add tuna, olives, feta and parsley; stir to combine. Serve the tuna salad over spinach.

SERVES 1: 1 cup tuna salad & 2 cups spinach

Calories 314 | **Fat** 21g (sat 5g) | **Cholesterol** 46mg | **Carbohydrates** 11g | **Total sugars** 2g (added 0g) | **Protein** 24g | **Fiber** 3g | **Sodium** 665mg | **Potassium** 543mg. **Nutrition bonus:** Vitamin A (113% daily value) | Vitamin C (41% dv) | Vitamin B$_{12}$ (40% dv) | Folate (29% dv) | Iron (26% dv) | Calcium (22% dv).

clean it up

Tuna contains varying levels of methylmercury, an environmental toxin that can have detrimental health effects in high amounts. Chunk light canned tuna is lower in mercury than albacore. You don't have to swear off albacore altogether, though—the FDA recommends limiting it to no more than 6 ounces per week to keep mercury levels in your overall diet low.

black-eyed pea dip

When pureed with extra-virgin olive oil, red-wine vinegar, garlic and thyme, black-eyed peas make an excellent alternative to hummus. Try this dip with your favorite sliced fresh vegetables or baked pita chips *(see Tip)*.

1 16-ounce can black-eyed peas, rinsed

2 tablespoons extra-virgin olive oil

2 teaspoons red-wine vinegar

1 clove garlic, minced

1 teaspoon dried thyme

Hot sauce to taste

Combine black-eyed peas, oil, vinegar, garlic, thyme and hot sauce in a blender or small food processor. Puree until smooth.

MAKES: 1¹⁄₂ cups (1-Tbsp. serving)

Calories 24 | Fat 1g (sat 0g) | Cholesterol 0mg | Carbohydrates 2g | Total sugars 0g (added 0g) | Protein 1g | Fiber 1g | Sodium 30mg | Potassium 27mg.

clean it up

To make your own toasted pita chips, cut 4 whole-wheat pita breads into 4 triangles each. Separate each triangle into 2 halves at the fold. Arrange, rough-side up, on a baking sheet. Spritz lightly with cooking spray or brush lightly with oil. Bake at 425°F until crisp, 8 to 10 minutes. Store in an airtight container at room temperature for up to 1 week or in the freezer for up to 2 months.

avocado-yogurt dip

Update your guacamole by adding tangy yogurt to it. For an extra kick, add minced jalapeño or a splash of your favorite hot sauce. Serve with vegetables, pita chips *(see Tip, page 210)* or baked tortilla chips, or use as a sandwich spread.

1 ripe avocado, pitted and peeled

¹/₂ cup nonfat plain yogurt

¹/₃ cup packed fresh cilantro leaves

2 tablespoons chopped onion

1 tablespoon lime juice

¹/₄ teaspoon salt

¹/₄ teaspoon ground pepper

Hot sauce to taste (optional)

Combine avocado, yogurt, cilantro, onion, lime juice, salt and pepper in a food processor. Process until smooth. Season with hot sauce, if desired.

MAKES: 1 cup (2-Tbsp. serving)

Calories 51 | Fat 4g (sat 1g) | Cholesterol 0mg | Carbohydrates 4g | Total sugars 1g (added 0g) | Protein 1g | Fiber 2g | Sodium 87mg | Potassium 171mg.

ACTIVE | 20 min
TOTAL | 30 min

To Make Ahead:
Loosely cover and refrigerate for up to 1 day.

classic deviled eggs

We love the tang of dill relish alongside minced shallot and Dijon in these. Our secret to healthy, creamy deviled eggs with fewer calories is to swap out half the full-fat mayo for nonfat Greek yogurt.

12 **large eggs**

¼ **cup nonfat plain Greek yogurt**

¼ **cup mayonnaise**

1 **tablespoon minced shallot**

1 **tablespoon dill relish** *(see Tip)*

2 **teaspoons Dijon mustard** *(see Tip)*

1 **teaspoon white-wine vinegar**

¼ **teaspoon salt**

¼ **teaspoon ground pepper**

⅛ **teaspoon paprika**

1. Place eggs in a single layer in a large pot; cover with water. Bring to a simmer over medium-high heat. Reduce heat to low and cook at the barest simmer for 10 minutes. Remove from heat, pour out the hot water and cover the eggs with ice-cold water. Let stand until cool enough to handle.

2. Peel the eggs and halve lengthwise with a sharp knife. Gently remove the yolks and place in a food processor. Add yogurt, mayonnaise, shallot, relish, mustard, vinegar, salt and pepper and process until smooth.

3. Spoon about 1 tablespoon of the filling into each egg white half. Just before serving, sprinkle with paprika.

SERVES 24: ½ egg each

Calories 47 | Fat 3g (sat 1g) | Cholesterol 94mg | Carbohydrates 1g | Total sugars 1g (added 0g) | Protein 3g | Fiber 0g | Sodium 83mg | Potassium 38mg.

clean it up

Unnecessary added sugar can lurk in many condiments. Opt for brands of Dijon mustard without it, and choose dill over sweet relish. If you're trying to avoid synthetic food dyes, be aware that some relishes contain Yellow 5 and/or Blue 1.

homemade trail mix

ACTIVE 5 min
TOTAL 5 min

To Make Ahead:
Store airtight at room
temperature for up to
2 weeks.

Try this portable mix with any combination of your favorite dried fruits and nuts, but make sure to choose unsweetened dried fruits.

¹/₄ cup whole shelled (unpeeled) almonds

¹/₄ **cup whole shelled (unpeeled) almonds**

¹/₄ **cup unsalted dry-roasted peanuts**

¹/₄ **cup unsweetened dried cherries** *(see Tip)*

¹/₄ **cup chopped pitted dates**

2 **ounces dried apricots** *or* **other dried fruit**

Combine almonds, peanuts, cherries, dates and apricots (or other fruit) in a medium bowl.

SERVES 5: about ¹/₄ cup each

Calories 150 | **Fat** 8g (sat 1g) | **Cholesterol** 0mg | **Carbohydrates** 20g | **Total sugars** 14g (added 0g) | **Protein** 4g | **Fiber** 3g | **Sodium** 5mg | **Potassium** 275mg.

 clean it up

Dried fruits (including sun-dried tomatoes) may be treated with sulfur dioxide to prevent spoilage and discoloration. It's a Generally Recognized As Safe (GRAS) additive per the FDA, but some people, particularly those with asthma, are sensitive to it, especially in larger amounts. In sensitive people, sulfites can cause allergy-like symptoms, such as hives, rash and/or breathing problems. To avoid it, read the ingredients label. Store sulfur-free dried fruit in the refrigerator or freezer to extend its shelf life. Also, choose dried fruit without added sweeteners.

ACTIVE 15 min

TOTAL 15 min

To Make Ahead:
Store airtight at room temperature or refrigerate for up to 1 week.

mango-date energy bites

Naturally sweet, sticky dates act as the "glue" for these no-cook snacks. They travel well, making them good for hikes or halftime breaks.

2 cups pitted whole dates

1 cup raw cashews

1 cup dried mango *or* other dried fruit

¼ teaspoon salt

Process dates, cashews, mango (or other fruit) and salt in a food processor until finely chopped. Form into about 20 balls, using 2 tablespoons each.

MAKES: 20 balls (1 per serving)

Calories 73 | **Fat** 3g (sat 1g) | **Cholesterol** 0mg | **Carbohydrates** 11g | **Total sugars** 9g (added 0g) | **Protein** 1g | **Fiber** 1g | **Sodium** 35mg | **Potassium** 78mg.

curried cashews

ACTIVE 5 min
TOTAL 50 min

To Make Ahead:
Store in an airtight
container for up to
3 weeks.

These baked curried cashews are impossibly addictive—be careful or they will disappear in a flash. Making them yourself cuts out the added sugar typically found in store-bought seasoned nuts. If you use salted cashews, omit the added salt.

6 tablespoons lemon juice

6 tablespoons curry powder

4 teaspoons kosher salt

6 cups unsalted cashews

1. Position racks in upper and lower thirds of oven; preheat to 250°F.

2. Whisk lemon juice, curry powder and salt in a large bowl. Add cashews; toss to coat. Divide between 2 large rimmed baking sheets; spread in an even layer.

3. Bake, stirring every 15 minutes, until dry, about 45 minutes. Let cool completely. Store in an airtight container.

MAKES: 6 cups (2-Tbsp. serving)

Calories 101 | Fat 8g (sat 2g) | Cholesterol 0mg | Carbohydrates 6g | Total sugars 1g (added 0g) | Protein 3g | Fiber 1g | Sodium 96mg | Potassium 107mg.

ACTIVE 5 min

TOTAL 5 min
(not including
popcorn-popping
time)

lemon-parmesan popcorn

A big bowl of popcorn makes a delightful snack, but it doesn't have to be boring. Perk it up with a sprinkle of lemon pepper and a touch of Parmesan cheese.

2 teaspoons extra-virgin olive oil

1/2 teaspoon lemon pepper *(see Tip)*

Pinch of salt

3 cups air-popped popcorn

1 tablespoon freshly grated Parmesan cheese

Whisk oil, lemon pepper and salt in a small bowl. Drizzle over popcorn and toss to coat. Sprinkle with Parmesan and serve immediately.

SERVES 2: 1¹/₂ cups each

Calories 99 | Fat 6g (sat 1g) | Cholesterol 2mg | Carbohydrates 10g | Total sugars 0g (added 0g) | Protein 2g | Fiber 2g | Sodium 199mg | Potassium 44mg.

clean it up

Spice blends like lemon pepper can contain added sugar. Check labels carefully or buy a sweetener-free version from a spice purveyor, such as *Penzeys.com*.

222   EATINGWELL QUICK + CLEAN

less sugar, more flavor desserts

Have a sweet tooth? If you love dessert, you should have it. But perhaps don't have it every day, and opt for treats that are lighter on sugar. In this chapter our approach to dessert is fruit-forward as opposed to sugar-forward, as in apricot grunt, blueberry cobbler and tart cherry sorbet. There's chocolate, too—occasionally it hits the spot like nothing else—so we've included an easy chocolate bark and a "chocomole" pudding made silky with avocado. The other thing you'll find here that you won't find with most desserts? They're 100% whole-grain. If you choose wisely, you can have your sweet treat without any guilt.

Apricot Grunt *(page 240)*

ACTIVE | 15 min
TOTAL | 45 min

To Make Ahead:
Refrigerate airtight for
up to 2 weeks.

cashew & 3-seed chocolate bark

In just a few simple steps, you can transform plain chocolate into a divine treat. Swap in other toasted nuts, like almonds or pecans, for the cashews or add a sprinkling of dried fruit, such as cranberries or chopped sour cherries.

2 cups chopped bittersweet *or* semisweet chocolate (*or* chips)

1/2 cup coarsely chopped cashews, lightly toasted (*see Tip, page 247*)

1/4 cup sunflower seeds, lightly toasted

1 tablespoon sesame seeds, lightly toasted

1 teaspoon aniseed, lighted toasted

1/4 teaspoon coarse salt

1. Line a rimmed baking sheet with foil. (Take care to avoid wrinkles.)

2. Place chocolate in a medium microwave-safe bowl; microwave on Medium for 1 minute. Stir, then continue microwaving on Medium, stirring every 20 seconds, until melted. (*Alternatively, place chocolate in the top of a double boiler over hot, but not boiling, water. Stir until melted.*)

3. Combine cashews, sunflower seeds, sesame seeds, aniseed and salt in a small bowl. Stir half of the mixture into the melted chocolate. Scrape the chocolate onto the foil and spread it into a 9-inch square. Sprinkle with the remaining cashew mixture, pressing any large bits in. Refrigerate until set, about 30 minutes.

4. Transfer the bark and foil to a cutting board. Use a sharp knife to cut into 1 1/2-inch pieces.

MAKES: 3 dozen 1 1/2-inch pieces (1 per serving)

Calories 59 | **Fat** 4g (sat 2g) | **Cholesterol** 0mg | **Carbohydrates** 7g | **Total sugars** 4g (added 3g) | **Protein** 1g | **Fiber** 1g | **Sodium** 14mg | **Potassium** 20mg.

To Make Ahead:
Refrigerate for up to 2 days.
Stir before serving.

"chocomole" pudding

Creamy avocados make this delicious dairy-free and vegan chocolate dessert super-rich. Serve with fresh raspberries or whole strawberries for dipping, if you like.

16 **Medjool dates, pitted and coarsely chopped**

1 **cup hot water**

3 **ripe avocados**

1 **cup unsweetened almond milk** *or* **coconut milk beverage**

1 **cup unsweetened cocoa powder**

1/4 **cup pure maple syrup** *or* **agave nectar**

1 **tablespoon coconut oil**

1 **teaspoon vanilla extract**

Pinch of sea salt, plus more for garnish

1. Soak dates in hot water until soft, 5 to 10 minutes. Drain.

2. Process the drained dates, avocados, milk beverage, cocoa, maple syrup (or agave), oil, vanilla and salt in a food processor until very smooth and creamy. Refrigerate until cold, about 3 hours. Serve garnished with a little extra sea salt, if desired.

SERVES 6: 1/2 cup each

Calories 434 | **Fat** 20g (sat 5g) | **Cholesterol** 0mg | **Carbohydrates** 74g | **Total sugars** 52g (added 8g) | **Protein** 6g | **Fiber** 16g | **Sodium** 54mg | **Potassium** 1,212mg. **Nutrition bonus:** Folate (24% daily value).

mascarpone-stuffed figs

Fresh figs are a voluptuous treat. Here, a creamy, honey-scented mascarpone filling adds to the luxury and yet still lets the fruit shine.

12 fresh ripe figs

$^1/_4$ cup mascarpone cheese

3 teaspoons honey, divided

1 teaspoon vanilla extract

2 tablespoons chopped almonds, toasted *(see Tip, page 247)*

1 teaspoon fresh mint, chopped

$^1/_2$ teaspoon orange zest

1. Trim about $^1/_2$ inch off the top of each fig. If needed, cut a thin slice off the bottom so they stand up straight. Cut an X into the tops about $^3/_4$ inch deep. Gently open each fig from the top without breaking it open all the way.

2. Combine mascarpone, 2 teaspoons honey and vanilla in a small bowl. Spoon about 1 teaspoon of the mixture into each fig. Drizzle with the remaining 1 teaspoon honey and sprinkle with almonds, mint and orange zest.

SERVES 4: 3 figs each

Calories 219 | **Fat** 15g (sat 7g) | **Cholesterol** 35mg | **Carbohydrates** 21g | **Total sugars** 18g (added 4g) | **Protein** 3g | **Fiber** 3g | **Sodium** 16mg | **Potassium** 225mg.

ACTIVE 25 min
TOTAL 25 min

caramelized spiced pears

These pear slices simmered in a spiced sauce are delectable served on their own or with a dollop of Greek yogurt. They also make a terrific topping for whole-grain pancakes or waffles. Brown-skinned Bosc pears hold their shape best during cooking, but any variety tastes delicious.

3 firm ripe pears (about 1½ pounds), cut into ¼-inch slices

1 tablespoon lemon juice

2 tablespoons unsalted butter

3 tablespoons granulated *or* light brown sugar

½ teaspoon ground cinnamon

½ teaspoon ground ginger

¼ teaspoon ground cloves

Pinch of salt

1. Toss pears with lemon juice in a medium bowl. Melt butter in a large deep skillet or large pot over medium heat; add the pears. Reduce heat to medium-low, cover and cook, stirring once halfway through, for 10 minutes.

2. Meanwhile, combine sugar, cinnamon, ginger, cloves and salt in a small bowl. After 10 minutes, stir the sugar mixture into the pears. Increase heat to medium and cook, stirring often, until the pears are tender and glazed, 4 to 6 minutes. Serve warm.

SERVES 6: about ½ cup each

Calories 111 | Fat 4g (sat 2g) | Cholesterol 10mg | Carbohydrates 20g | Total sugars 15g (added 6g) | Protein 0g | Fiber 3g | Sodium 26mg | Potassium 111mg.

double corn-blueberry cobbler

The hallmark of a cobbler is a biscuit topping baked right on top of the fruit. Here we match up blueberries with cornbread biscuits. The batter looks stunning on top of the deep-dark fruit filling. We like the rustic texture of medium- or coarse-ground cornmeal, but any type works. Most of the sweetness in this dessert comes from the fruit and corn, rather than added sugar.

FILLING

4 cups blueberries *or* blackberries (about 1¹/₄ pounds), fresh *or* frozen, thawed

¹/₄ cup sugar

1 tablespoon white whole-wheat flour

¹/₄ teaspoon grated lemon zest

1 tablespoon lemon juice

TOPPING

1 cup white whole-wheat flour

³/₄ cup cornmeal, preferably medium- or coarse-ground

1¹/₂ teaspoons baking powder

¹/₄ teaspoon baking soda

¹/₄ teaspoon salt

1 large egg yolk

¹/₂ cup buttermilk

¹/₄ cup canola oil

3 tablespoons sugar

¹/₂ cup corn kernels, fresh, frozen (thawed) or canned (well-drained)

1. Preheat oven to 375°F.

2. **To prepare filling:** Combine berries, ¹/₄ cup sugar, 1 tablespoon flour, lemon zest and lemon juice in a large bowl. Transfer to a 9-inch shallow glass or ceramic baking dish.

3. **To prepare topping:** Whisk flour, cornmeal, baking powder, baking soda and salt in a large bowl until well blended. Whisk egg yolk, buttermilk, oil and sugar in a small bowl. Add the wet ingredients to the dry ingredients and stir to combine. Fold in corn.

4. Evenly spoon the batter on top of the berry mixture. Place the baking dish on a baking sheet to catch any drips. Bake until the filling is bubbling, the topping is golden brown and a toothpick inserted into the center of the topping comes out clean, 35 to 50 minutes. Let cool for about 20 minutes before serving.

SERVES 8: about ³/₄ cup each

Calories 263 | Fat 8g (sat 1g) | Cholesterol 24mg | Carbohydrates 45g | Total sugars 20g (added 11g) | Protein 5g | Fiber 4g | Sodium 240mg | Potassium 163mg.

spiced apple bread pudding

A boost of flavor from fresh apple slices tossed with plenty of spices helps keep the sugar to a minimum in this homey dessert. Vanilla-spiked apple cider replaces the custard common in many bread puddings. To stale bread naturally, store it at room temperature in a paper (not plastic) bag for 2 to 5 days or bake cubed bread at 250°F until crisped and dry, 15 to 20 minutes.

1¹/₂ **pounds tart apples (3-4 medium), such as Granny Smith, Empire *or* Cortland**

2 **tablespoons light brown sugar**

1 **teaspoon ground cinnamon**

¹/₂ **teaspoon ground mace *or* nutmeg**

3 **cups apple cider**

2 **tablespoons unsalted butter, melted**

1 **teaspoon vanilla extract**

6 **cups 1-inch pieces stale whole-wheat bread without crust**

¹/₃ **cup golden raisins**

¹/₂ **cup walnuts, toasted (*see Tip, page 247*) and chopped**

1. Preheat oven to 350°F.

2. Peel and thinly slice apples. Toss with brown sugar, cinnamon and mace (or nutmeg) in a medium bowl. Combine cider, butter and vanilla in another medium bowl.

3. Cover the bottom of a 3-quart round casserole dish (or similar-size pan) with 2 cups bread pieces. Pour about ¹/₂ cup of the cider mixture over them. Sprinkle with about one-third of the raisins and cover with about one-third of the apple slices. Repeat with another layer of 2 cups bread, ¹/₂ cup cider and half the remaining raisins and apple slices. For the third layer, arrange the rest of the bread, raisins and apples so that some of each is visible on the surface. Slowly ladle the remaining cider mixture over the top. Using a flat, wide spatula, press down to compact and submerge the top layer (it may not remain submerged). Cover with a lid or foil.

4. Bake for 30 minutes. Use the spatula again to press down the top and baste it with the liquid. Cover and bake for 30 minutes more. Baste the top layer again by pressing down on it with the spatula. Keep the cover off and continue baking until the top is golden, about 30 minutes more. Let rest on a wire rack for 15 minutes.

5. Scoop the pudding into individual serving dishes. Sprinkle each portion with some of the nuts.

SERVES 8: ²/₃ cup each

Calories 259 | Fat 9g (sat 2g) | Cholesterol 8mg | Carbohydrates 42g | Total sugars 26g (added 5g) | Protein 6g | Fiber 4g | Sodium 132mg | Potassium 236mg.

mini blueberry-lemon cheesecakes

ACTIVE 35 min

TOTAL 3 hrs 10 min
(including 2 hrs
cooling & chilling
time)

To Make Ahead:
Loosely cover and refrigerate
for up to 1 day.

Equipment: 2 muffin tins
with 12 (1/2-cup) cups

These fruit-forward ricotta cheesecakes are bursting with zesty flavor and are surprisingly low in added sugar. Baked in muffin cups, they are easy to store and can be made a day in advance.

1 1/2 cups graham cracker crumbs (from about 10 whole graham crackers)

3 tablespoons canola oil

1 15-ounce container part-skim ricotta cheese (see *Tip*)

2 8-ounce packages reduced-fat cream cheese (see *Tip*), at room temperature

4 large eggs

1 cup granulated sugar

2 teaspoons grated lemon zest

5 tablespoons lemon juice

1 teaspoon vanilla extract

1/2 teaspoon salt

1 1/2 cups blueberries, fresh *or* frozen (not thawed), divided

1. Preheat oven to 325°F. Line 24 (1/2-cup) muffin cups with paper liners or coat with cooking spray.

2. Combine graham cracker crumbs and oil in a small bowl. Press about 2 teaspoons into the bottom of each muffin cup.

3. Beat ricotta in a large bowl with an electric mixer until smooth. Add cream cheese, eggs, sugar, lemon zest and juice, vanilla and salt; beat until smooth. Fold in 1 cup blueberries. Spoon about 1/4 cup cheesecake batter into each muffin cup. Sprinkle each cheesecake with some of the remaining blueberries.

4. Bake the cheesecakes until almost set in the center, 32 to 35 minutes. Let cool in the pans on a wire rack until room temperature, about 1 hour. Loosely cover with plastic wrap and refrigerate until cold, at least 2 hours and up to 1 day.

SERVES 24: 1 cheesecake each

Calories 166 | Fat 9g (sat 4g) | Cholesterol 50mg | Carbohydrates 17g | Total sugars 12g (added 10g) | Protein 5g | Fiber 0g | Sodium 170mg | Potassium 84mg.

clean it up

Glance at the ingredient lists of part-skim ricotta and reduced-fat cream cheese and you'll notice many contain stabilizers like gums and carrageenan. These stabilizers do just that—stabilize the texture of the products, keeping them from separating, and making them creamier and smoother. The stabilizing gums are usually harmless, but since carrageenan may be linked to inflammation in the gut, you may want to skip brands that contain it.

apricot grunt

In this easy summertime dessert, apricots simmer in a skillet with honey and a touch of cloves and are topped with whole-grain buttermilk biscuits. Try it with any type or combination of fruit—frozen works well too. Use a nonreactive pan, such as stainless-steel or enamel-coated, to prevent the acidic fruit from reacting with the pan; aluminum and cast-iron pans can impart off colors and flavors. *(Photo: page 224.)*

FILLING

  6 cups sliced ripe apricots, nectarines *or* **peaches (**^{1}/$_2$**-inch slices), peeled if desired, fresh** *or* **frozen**

^{1}/$_3$ **cup honey**

  2 teaspoons lemon juice

^{1}/$_8$ **teaspoon ground cloves**

TOPPING

^{1}/$_2$ **cup white whole-wheat flour**

  2 tablespoons sugar plus 1 teaspoon, divided

^{1}/$_2$ **teaspoon baking powder**

^{1}/$_4$ **teaspoon baking soda**

^{1}/$_4$ **teaspoon salt**

^{1}/$_4$ **cup buttermilk**

  1 tablespoon canola oil

^{1}/$_4$ **teaspoon ground cinnamon**

1. To prepare filling: Combine fruit, honey, lemon juice and cloves in a 10-inch nonreactive skillet with a lid. Bring to a boil, uncovered, stirring frequently. Reduce heat to a gentle simmer and cook, uncovered, until starting to soften, about 5 minutes.

2. To prepare topping: Whisk flour, 2 tablespoons sugar, baking powder, baking soda and salt in a medium bowl. Whisk buttermilk and oil in a measuring cup. Gradually drizzle the buttermilk mixture over the dry ingredients, tossing with a fork just until evenly moistened. Mix the remaining 1 teaspoon sugar with cinnamon in a small bowl.

3. Drop 6 equal portions of batter (about 1 generous tablespoon each) onto the surface of the bubbling fruit. Sprinkle with the cinnamon sugar.

4. Cover the pan and cook for 15 minutes without lifting the lid. If the biscuits are not set, replace the lid and cook until set, about 5 minutes more. The biscuits should be puffed and firm to the touch. Let cool, uncovered, for about 20 minutes before serving.

SERVES 6

Calories 194 | Fat 3g (sat 0g) | **Cholesterol** 0mg | **Carbohydrates** 42g | **Total sugars** 32g (added 20g) | **Protein** 3g | **Fiber** 4g | **Sodium** 213mg | **Potassium** 359mg. **Nutrition bonus:** Vitamin A (47% daily value) | Vitamin C (22% dv).

To Make Ahead:
Freeze in an airtight
container for up to 1 week.

cherry sorbet

This sorbet is great on its own, or spruce it up with a dollop of whipped cream and a sprinkle of chopped fresh or dried cherries. Use this same method with other fruits, such as strawberries or sliced peaches.

4 cups pitted sour *or* sweet cherries *(see Tip, page 247)*, fresh *or* frozen (not thawed)

1 cup water

2-4 tablespoons confectioners' sugar *or* superfine sugar

Puree cherries, water and sugar to taste in a blender until smooth. Strain through a fine sieve, pressing on the solids to extract as much liquid as possible. (Discard solids.) If you have an ice cream maker, process according to the manufacturer's directions until firm and slushy. (If not, pour the strained mixture into a 9-by-13-inch baking pan and place it on a level surface in your freezer; stir and scrape with a fork every 30 minutes, moving the frozen edges in toward the center and crushing any lumps, until firm and slushy, 2½ to 3 hours.) Transfer to an airtight container and freeze until ready to serve.

SERVES 8: about ½ cup each

Calories 46 | **Fat** 0g (sat 0g) | **Cholesterol** 0mg | **Carbohydrates** 11g | **Total sugars** 8g (added 2g) | **Protein** 1g | **Fiber** 1g | **Sodium** 3mg | **Potassium** 134mg. **Nutrition bonus:** Vitamin A (20% daily value).

To Make Ahead:
Freeze airtight for up to
1 week; let stand at room
temperature to soften
slightly before serving.

instant mango
frozen yogurt

Blend frozen mango and Greek yogurt to create a luscious dessert that couldn't be simpler.
To make this with fresh mango, peel and dice enough fruit to make 4^1/$_2$ cups. Spread on a baking
sheet in a single layer and freeze until solid.

**4^1/$_2$ cups diced frozen mango (16-ounce bag),
not thawed**

1^1/$_2$ cups nonfat plain Greek yogurt

^{1}/$_3$ cup confectioners' sugar *or* **brown sugar**

Combine mango, yogurt and sugar in a food
processor. Process until smooth.

SERVES 6: ^{1}/$_2$ cup each

Calories 107 | **Fat** 0g (sat 0g) | **Cholesterol** 3mg |
Carbohydrates 22g | **Total sugars** 20g (added 6g) |
Protein 6g | **Fiber** 2g | **Sodium** 20mg | **Potassium** 79mg.
Nutrition bonus: Vitamin C (32% daily value).

At EatingWell we aim to create recipes that taste absolutely delicious and work perfectly every time. They also adhere to guidelines for healthful eating. To that end, we perfect each recipe we publish through rigorous testing—and provide accurate nutritional information so you can make informed decisions about what you eat. Here's how we do it.

HOW WE TEST RECIPES

- Recipes are tested in the *EatingWell* Test Kitchen on average seven times each by multiple testers—both home cooks and culinary-school graduates.

- We test on both gas and electric stoves.

- We use a variety of tools and techniques.

- Testers shop at major supermarkets to research availability of ingredients.

- Testers measure active and total time to prepare each recipe.

- "Active" time includes prep time (the time it takes to chop, dice, puree, mix, combine, etc., before cooking begins), but it also includes the time spent tending something on the stovetop, in the oven or on the grill—and getting it to the table. If you can't walk away from it, we consider it active minutes.

- "Total" includes both active and inactive minutes and indicates the entire amount of time required for each recipe, start to finish.

- "To Make Ahead" gives storage instructions to help you plan. If particular "Equipment" is needed, we tell you that at the top of the recipe too.

HOW WE ANALYZE RECIPES

- All recipes are analyzed for nutrition content by a registered dietitian.

- We analyze for calories, total fat, saturated (sat) fat, cholesterol, carbohydrates, total sugars, added sugars, protein, fiber, sodium and potassium using The Food Processor® SQL Nutrition Analysis Software from ESHA Research, Salem, Oregon.

- Garnishes and optional ingredients are not included in analyses.

- When a recipe gives a measurement range of an ingredient, we analyze the first amount.

- When alternative ingredients are listed, we analyze the first one suggested.

- Recipes are tested and analyzed with iodized table salt unless otherwise indicated.

- We estimate that rinsing certain canned foods (like beans) with water reduces the sodium by 35 percent. (Readers on sodium-restricted diets can reduce or eliminate the added salt in a recipe.)

- To help people eat in accordance with the USDA's Dietary Guidelines, *EatingWell*'s suggested portions generally are based upon standard serving sizes. For example, suggested servings for meat, poultry and fish are generally 3 to 4 ounces, cooked. A recommended portion of a starch-based side dish, such as rice or potatoes, is generally ½ cup. Vegetable side dishes are a minimum of ½ cup.

- When a recipe provides 20 percent or more of the Daily Value (dv) of a nutrient, it is listed as a nutrition bonus. These values are FDA benchmarks for adults eating 2,000 calories a day.

- For more on our nutritional-analysis process, visit *eatingwell.com/eatingwell_nutrition_and_recipe_guidelines*.

Techniques & Notes

- To make **breadcrumbs:** For fresh breadcrumbs, trim crusts from whole-wheat bread, tear the bread into pieces and process in a food processor until coarse crumbs form. (To make fine breadcrumbs, process until very fine.) For coarse dry breadcrumbs, spread the coarse crumbs on a baking sheet and bake at 250°F until dry, 10 to 15 minutes. (One slice of bread makes about ⅓ cup dry breadcrumbs.)

- To pit **cherries:** Use a tool made for the job—a hand-held cherry pitter; it also works for olives! Or pry out the pit with the tip of a knife or vegetable peeler.

- To poach **chicken breast:** Place boneless, skinless chicken breasts in a skillet or saucepan. Add lightly salted water to cover and bring to a boil. Cover, reduce heat to a simmer and cook until no longer pink in the middle, 10 to 15 minutes, depending on size. (Eight ounces raw boneless, skinless chicken breast yields about 1 cup sliced, diced or shredded cooked chicken.)

- To toast **coconut:** Place coconut chips or flakes in a small dry skillet over medium-low heat and cook, stirring constantly, until light brown in spots, 4 to 8 minutes.

- To skin a **fish fillet,** place it on a clean cutting board, skin-side down. Starting at the tail end, slip the blade of a long, sharp knife between the fish flesh and the skin, holding the skin down firmly with your other hand. Gently push the blade along at a 30° angle, separating the fillet from the skin without cutting through either.

- To cook **lentils:** Place in a saucepan, cover with at least 1 inch of water, bring to a simmer and cook until just tender, 15 to 30 minutes, depending on the type of lentil. Drain and rinse with cold water. One cup dry lentils yields about 2½ cups cooked. Or use canned lentils: a 15-ounce can yields 1½ cups. Rinse canned lentils before cooking with them to reduce the sodium by about 35 percent.

- Use **nonreactive** bowls or pans—stainless-steel, enamel-coated, nonstick or glass—when cooking with acidic foods (citrus, berries, tomatoes) to prevent the food from reacting with the dish. Reactive cookware (aluminum and cast-iron) can impart off colors and/or flavors.

- To toast **nuts and seeds:** Toast small nuts, chopped or sliced nuts or seeds in a small dry skillet over medium-low heat, stirring constantly, until fragrant and lightly browned, 2 to 4 minutes. Spread whole nuts on a baking sheet and bake at 350°F, stirring once, until fragrant and lightly browned, 7 to 9 minutes.

- To make lean ground **pork:** Depending on your supermarket, it might be hard to find a lean option for ground pork. But it's easy to make your own in a food processor. Choose a lean cut, such as loin or tenderloin. Cut into pieces and pulse in a food processor until uniformly ground (being careful not to overprocess, turning the meat into mush). Or ask your butcher to grind it for you. Using lean pork instead of regular ground pork saves up to 164 calories and 5 grams of saturated fat per 3 ounces of cooked meat.

EatingWell Buyer's Guides

Labels on food packaging can be confusing. The following guides will help you interpret them so you can choose poultry, meat, seafood and eggs that are fresh, free of unwanted additives and raised using the standards for sustainability and humane treatment that you're looking for.

POULTRY

The best way to ensure you're buying the freshest poultry is to look at the fat—it should be white to deep yellow, never gray or pale. Make sure the package is well wrapped and leak-free.

Check the label carefully to avoid poultry that has been "enhanced" with an added sodium solution—it's higher in sodium than those without added solution. The word "natural" on the label does not guarantee a nonenhanced product. To determine if poultry is enhanced, scan the ingredients on the label for any added solution that is not plain water.

Refrigerate or freeze poultry as soon as possible after purchase. If refrigerating, be sure to cook it or freeze it by the "use by" date on the package. If you're freezing poultry for longer than two weeks, make sure it is wrapped tightly, either in a vacuum-sealed package, heavy-duty foil, freezer paper or in a freezer bag. Frozen poultry should be defrosted in the refrigerator, never at room temperature, to prevent bacterial growth.

Here are some of the most common ways that poultry is labeled and marketed, along with definitions of what those words mean:

- **Free-Range:** While it might seem to imply more, this USDA-regulated term means only that the birds are granted access to the outdoors.

- **Certified Organic:** This USDA-regulated term means that all feed must be certified organic: no synthetic fertilizers or pesticides, animal by-products or other additives. Certified organic poultry must also meet "free-range" criteria.

- **Raised Without Antibiotics:** This term indicates that the birds were raised without antibiotics for health maintenance, disease prevention or treatment of disease. Medications not classified as antibiotics may still be used.

- **No Hormones:** The USDA prohibits the use of hormones in poultry, so while the label "hormone-free" is accurate, it doesn't set one poultry product apart from another.

- **Natural:** One of the most widely used labels, the term means that no additives or preservatives were introduced after the poultry was processed (although certain sodium-based broths can be added; read the ingredients on the package label if this is a concern). "Natural" has absolutely nothing to do with standards of care, type and quality of feed or administration of medications.

- **Vegetarian-Fed or All-Vegetable Diet:** The birds were fed a diet containing no animal products. This is a controversial practice because chickens and turkeys are not naturally vegetarian, and poultry feed usually includes some meat and poultry by-products. Also, the birds naturally like to forage for insects when they are able.

- **Percent Retained Water:** To control pathogens like *Salmonella*, producers must quickly lower the temperature of meat during processing. Most do this by immersing the slaughtered birds in a cold bath, which causes them to absorb water. The USDA requires producers to list the maximum amount of water that may be retained.

- **Air Chilled:** Some producers lower the temperature of meat during processing using an extremely cold blast of air. This process does not result in any retained water.

- **Certified Humane Raised & Handled:** Overseen by the nonprofit group Humane Farm Animal Care (*certifiedhumane.org*), this label ensures the birds received certain basic standards of care and were encouraged to engage in natural behaviors, such as perching, pecking and scratching, and foraging for food in their bedding. If also labeled "Free-Range" or "Pasture-Raised," the birds must have been raised to these standards as well.

- **Farm-Raised:** This is not a regulated label, so it can technically be used on almost any poultry products.

- **Pasture-Raised:** This is not a regulated label, but Humane Farm Animal Care has created a standard for the term that it guarantees. Birds must be outdoors year-round, with access to housing where they can go inside to protect themselves from predators or extreme weather.

BEEF

When buying beef there are many choices to make besides what cut to use. This includes what the animal was fed, what medications it might have been given and how it was treated during its life. This guide covers what to look for at the market, how to understand the package labels and what to ask when you're buying beef at a farmers' market or directly from the farmer.

Fresh beef should be bright red. Occasional gray or brownish discoloration caused by oxidization can be unappealing but is safe to eat. Vacuum-packaged beef will be maroon because of the lack of oxygen. The meat should be firm to the touch with little to no excess moisture in the package, and the packaging should be in good condition. Avoid beef that has a bad odor or is sticky or slimy to the touch. Finally, be sure to check the "use by" date.

Refrigerate or freeze beef as soon as possible after purchase. Be sure to cook it or freeze it by the "use by" date on the package. If you're freezing beef for longer than two weeks, make sure it is wrapped tightly, either in a vacuum-sealed package, heavy-duty foil, freezer paper or in a freezer bag. Frozen beef should be defrosted in the refrigerator, never at room temperature, to prevent bacterial growth.

Here are some of the most common ways that beef is labeled and marketed, along with definitions of what those words mean:

- **Prime, Choice or Select:** The USDA assigns a quality grade to beef, determined by the amount of marbling and the age of the animal, both of which affect the tenderness, juiciness and flavor of the meat. Prime meat has the most marbling (fat) within the meat, making it juicy and flavorful but also increasing its fat content; Select has the least marbling; Choice is in the middle.

- **Raised Without Antibiotics:** This term indicates that the animal wasn't given antibiotics to prevent or treat a disease or to promote growth.

- **No Hormones:** Producers who show documentation that they do not use hormones to promote growth when raising their cattle may use this label.

- **Natural:** One of the most widely used labels, the term means only that the meat has been minimally processed and doesn't contain any artificial ingredients or preservatives. "Natural" doesn't address standards of care, type and quality of feed or administration of medications.

- **Percent Retained Water:** To control pathogens like *Salmonella*, producers must quickly lower the temperature of meat during processing. Most do this by immersing the slaughtered animals in a cold bath, which causes them to absorb water. The USDA requires producers to list the maximum amount of water that may be retained.

- **Certified Organic:** This USDA-regulated term means that all feed given to cattle must be certified organic, which means no synthetic fertilizers, pesticides, animal by-products or other additives. Farmers cannot use antibiotics or growth-promoting hormones on cattle raised to meet certified organic standards. The animals also must have access to pasture.

- **Certified Humane Raised & Handled:** Overseen by a nonprofit endorsed by the American Society for the Prevention of Cruelty to Animals and the Humane Society of the United States, this label ensures the animal received basic standards of care. For example, in conditions of extreme heat, sun shades and water-cooling systems must be available to cattle. Feed must be fresh. Cattle must have sufficient room to lie down in their normal positions in a clean area.

- **Grass-Fed:** "Grass-fed" on a label is no longer a USDA-regulated term, but there are third-party groups that certify how cattle are fed. The American Grassfed Association's third-party-certified logo goes beyond by indicating not only that cattle are 100 percent grass-fed, but also that they were raised without hormones or antibiotics, were not confined and were raised humanely. The Food Alliance logo also certifies grass-fed claims.

- **Grain-Finished, Grass-Finished, Pastured:** These terms are unregulated.

PORK

Look for pork that is light red to cherry red, never pale or white. The fat should be white and creamy with no dark spots. Fresh pork should never have any off odors. The best-tasting pork is marbled with flecks of fat interspersed in the lean meat.

Avoid pale, soft pork sitting in the package in liquid—it indicates pork that comes from animals stressed during processing. The meat will be dry and tasteless even when cooked to the desired degree of doneness.

Because lean pork can dry out so quickly when cooked, many manufacturers sell something called "enhanced" pork. It is injected with a solution of water, salt and phosphates. The percentage of water is usually around 8 to 10 percent. It can have a soft, rubbery texture and a slightly acrid or bitter taste. To determine if pork is enhanced, check the label for any added solution that is not plain water.

Refrigerate or freeze pork as soon as possible after purchase. Be sure to cook it or freeze it by the "use by" date on the package. If you're freezing pork for longer than two weeks, make sure it is wrapped tightly, either in a vacuum-sealed package, heavy-duty foil, freezer paper or in a freezer bag. Frozen pork should be defrosted in the refrigerator, never at room temperature, to prevent bacterial growth.

Here are some of the most common ways that pork is labeled and marketed, along with definitions of what those words mean:

- **Certified Organic:** This USDA-regulated term means that all feed given to the pigs must be certified organic, which means no synthetic fertilizers, pesticides, animal by-products or other additives. Pigs raised to meet certified organic standards also must have access to pasture.

- **Raised Without Antibiotics:** This term indicates that the pork was raised without any use of antibiotics (commonly used for health maintenance, disease prevention or treatment of disease). Medications not classified as antibiotics may still be used.

- **No Hormones:** The USDA prohibits the use of hormones in pigs, so while the label "hormone-free" is accurate, it doesn't set one pork product apart from another.

- **Natural:** One of the most widely used labels, this simply means that no additives or preservatives were introduced after the pork was processed. "Natural" doesn't tell you anything about standards of care, type and quality of feed or administration of medications.

- **Percent Retained Water:** To control pathogens like *Salmonella*, producers must quickly lower the temperature of meat during processing. Most do this by immersing the slaughtered animals in a cold bath, which causes them to absorb water. The USDA requires producers to list the maximum amount of water that may be retained.

- **Certified Humane Raised & Handled:** Overseen by a nonprofit endorsed by the American Society for the Prevention of Cruelty to Animals and the Humane Society, this label ensures the animal received the basic standards of care that are regulated by the USDA. Encouraging natural behaviors is also considered: pigs must have access to straw or other material to root around in, as well as objects for manipulation, such as chains or balls.

SEAFOOD

Seafood is an excellent source of lean protein. And some types of fish, particularly cold-water species like salmon, tuna, sardines and trout, are rich in two important omega-3 fatty acids, docosahexaenoic acid (DHA) and eicosapentaenoic acid (EPA). Studies show that these omega-3 fats may reduce the risk of heart disease and may also provide other health benefits, such as helping to prevent Alzheimer's disease and boost your mood. But choosing fish means navigating other health and environmental concerns.

One health concern is mercury, but for most people the benefits of eating fish outweigh risk from the methylmercury that's found in varying levels in seafood. In general, the larger (and older) the fish, the higher in mercury it will be (the metal accumulates over time, especially in fish high on the food chain that eat smaller fish). High levels of mercury can cause tingling or numbness in fingers and toes and vision problems, and can affect infant brain development. Even consistent, low-level mercury exposure can leave you fatigued or make concentrating difficult. The USDA's Dietary Guidelines say to eat at least 8 ounces of seafood a week—choosing lower-mercury fish (salmon, shrimp, canned light tuna, tilapia, cod) and some omega-3-rich fish. Follow these guidelines and you should be fine.

So where's the line of "too much"? If you cook up a high-mercury fish (tilefish, shark, swordfish, albacore tuna, king mackerel) even just once a month, some say you might get too much mercury. And a 2016 Environmental Working Group report found that eating tuna steaks, sushi tuna, sea bass, halibut and marlin could also be risky. Still, there's no clear cutoff. Women who are or may become pregnant or are breast-feeding, and young children should avoid high-mercury fish.

Making an eco-friendly choice varies according to the type of fish, where it's from and whether it's wild or farmed. At the fish counter, you should see country-of-origin labeling, now required by federal law. For help making informed choices, and for the most up-to-date information, check the websites of several expert sources, including Monterey Bay Aquarium's Seafood Watch, the Marine Stewardship Council and The Safina Center. Also good to know when fish shopping: most wild-caught fish is frozen at sea, so frozen or previously frozen fish is often the "freshest" you'll find. Fish should look moist and firm and should have a mild smell.

Here's how to shop for some of the most commonly eaten fish and shellfish:

catfish

Most catfish on the U.S. market is farmed and, when raised in recirculating systems or in U.S. ponds, is considered a good choice. Pangasius, a farmed catfish imported from Vietnam, Cambodia and China, is popular in Asian restaurants and may also be called basa, swai, tra or sutchi. You may see it frozen or previously frozen at the fish counter. Unless pangasius has a Marine Stewardship Council seal, it likely was raised using intensive pond-farming practices that are environmentally destructive and potentially unhealthy, according to Seafood Watch. In addition, there have been concerns about antibiotic use in foreign catfish farming. However, according to *seafoodhealthfacts.org* (another helpful source for deciding what fish to buy), practices are improving thanks to consumer demand for eco-friendly fish.

cod & pollock

Cod are a versatile white fish and are mostly wild-caught (farming is just being developed for these species) but have problems with many of their fisheries, including overfishing and excess bycatch. Atlantic cod stocks are particularly depleted. Pacific cod or eco-friendly farmed Atlantic cod (in tank-based systems) are the best choices.

Alaskan pollock is the largest U.S. wild fishery. The National Oceanic and Atmospheric Administration says

these fisheries are well-managed, but Seafood Watch recommends that you choose products with the Marine Stewardship Council's blue checkmark label.

salmon

A fatty fish, salmon is especially high in omega-3s and has become a go-to dinner choice for good reason. Most wild salmon is considered a sustainable choice.

Farmed Atlantic salmon is widely available and affordable, and its omega-3 levels are comparable to those of wild salmon. Large and high in fat, this salmon is full-flavored, moist and very versatile for cooking. But many farmed salmon are not considered a sustainable choice, due to farming systems that pollute surrounding waters and threaten wild fish populations. Look for fish raised in land- or tank-based systems, which are better for the environment than most traditional open-net farms. Seek out farmed salmon that have a third-party certification for sustainability, such as the Global Aquaculture Alliance's Best Aquaculture Practices. Look for their logo on packages. There is no regulated organic standard for salmon, so if you do see an "organic" label, it doesn't necessarily mean anything.

tilapia

A freshwater fish that originated in North Africa, tilapia can now be found at fish counters across the U.S., where its mild taste and light white meat have made it so popular that it's been nicknamed "aqua chicken."

Since tilapia is an herbivorous fish, tilapia farms don't need to use wild fish for feed, minimizing some of the environmental impact. And tilapia actually help clean the water by eating algae. Look for North American farm-raised tilapia, grown in closed farming systems that limit fish-waste pollution and prevent escapes of the farmed fish into the wild. Some Central and South American tilapia farms used closed systems as well, but tilapia from China and Taiwan may have more negative impacts, because pollution and antibiotic use aren't as well regulated in these countries and the farms are open to surrounding waters.

tuna

A warm-water fatty fish, tuna is found throughout the world's seas. Yellowfin and bigeye tuna, also called ahi, are common at supermarket fish counters. Yellowfin and skipjack are what you'll usually find canned under the "chunk light" label.

Tuna is high in omega-3s, but can also be high in mercury, since these big fish eat high on the food chain. Those who need to be concerned about mercury (pregnant and breast-feeding women, and growing children) should opt for smaller species—look for yellowfin (ahi) tuna at your seafood counter and choose canned chunk light tuna, rather than white (albacore). Avoid bluefin tuna, used mostly in sushi and sashimi: stocks of these huge fish are severely depleted, and the methods used to catch them endanger other sea creatures, such as sea turtles and sharks.

clams

Clams are a stellar choice for two reasons: these bivalves are especially high in B vitamins as well as minerals, such as selenium, zinc and magnesium, and they represent one of the few truly environmentally friendly fisheries. Natural stocks are healthy and sufficient to meet demand, farms are well-managed, and clams' active filtering can improve the waters they grow in. Most clams get a "best choice" rating from Seafood Watch.

Check to make sure whole, in-shell clams are alive (shells should be closed or close when you tap them). People at high risk for foodborne illness should avoid eating raw clams. If a recipe calls for chopped clams, look for them fresh or frozen in the seafood department: compared to canned, they have a higher clam-to-liquid ratio and are lower in sodium. Canned baby clams also work well in many recipes.

crab

Look for crab in the seafood department of large supermarkets. "Jumbo" or "lump" crabmeat is higher quality, with a sweeter taste, more toothsome bite and larger pieces; claw meat is a budget–friendly option. If you live in an area known for crab, you may be able to get live or freshly cooked crabs at the seafood counter of your local market.

Most U.S. crab is considered sustainable, but Seafood Watch advises being wary of crab labeled "Atlantic rock crab" (from New England)—a label that's fine when authentic but that's often used on other types from poorly managed fisheries. Crab from Canada, Australia and Norway is usually a good choice, but other imported crab, often sold canned from Southeast Asia, should be avoided.

scallops

Sea scallops are larger and are great for sautéing or broiling. Try the smaller bay scallops in soups or tossed in a pasta sauce. Both farmed and wild scallops are a sustainable choice.

We recommend cooking with "dry" sea scallops (scallops that have not been treated with sodium tripolyphosphate, or STP). Scallops that have been treated with STP ("wet" scallops) have been subjected to a chemical bath and are not only often mushy and less flavorful, but also will not brown properly because they'll give off too much liquid. Dry sea scallops are often labeled as such.

shrimp

Raw, frozen and cooked shrimp are all sold by the number needed to make 1 pound—for example, "21-25 count" or "31-40 count"—and by more generic size names, such as "large" or "extra large." Size names don't always correspond to the actual "count size." To be sure you're getting the size you want, order by the count (or number) per pound.

Shrimp's popularity has led to environmental problems from intense farming and fishing. Both wild-caught and farm-raised shrimp can damage surrounding ecosystems. Fortunately, it is possible to buy shrimp that have been raised or caught with sound environmental practices. Look for shrimp that's certified by an agency like the Marine Stewardship Council. If you can't find it, choose wild-caught shrimp from North America—it's more likely to be sustainably caught.

For best taste and health, limit preservatives that are often used by processors when freezing shrimp. You can see if they've been used by reading the package label. Here are the three to watch out for:

- Sodium bisulfite is considered safe by the FDA, though some people are sensitive to it. It's only required to be on the label when it exceeds 10 parts per million.
- Sodium tripolyphosphate (STP) bulks up shrimp, causing them to shrink when cooked. It boosts sodium levels by more than four times in some brands. To figure out how heavily treated your shrimp is, check the label and compare it to this baseline: untreated raw shrimp has a sodium count of about 250 mg for every 100 grams.
- Everfresh is also used as a preservative to control black spots. It's made of 4-hexylresorcinol, a compound with antiseptic properties (also in throat lozenges). The FDA considers it safe. It doesn't require labeling and is accepted by most organic retailers. But a recent study showed 4-hexylresorcinol can be considered a xenoestrogen, which at high levels may boost estrogen levels, increasing the risk of breast cancer in women.

EGGS

Choosing eggs has gotten pretty complicated. First, there's color. While you may find some pretty eggs, especially from small farms or at the farmers' market, there's no inherent nutritional or taste difference. The hen's breed determines the egg color.

Then, there are labels. If you're buying eggs at a supermarket, you may see the following terms on the carton. (If you're buying from a farm or farmers' market, ask the farmer about the chickens' diet and welfare.)

- **Cage-Free:** Per the USDA, these eggs come from hens that are housed in a "building, room or enclosed area that allows for unlimited access to food, water and provides freedom to roam within the area during the laying cycle." There are no requirements for the minimum amount of space per hen or any outdoor access, or for comforts like perches or nest boxes.

- **Date:** Most egg cartons have a "sell by" or "packed on" date printed on the end. Eggs stored in their carton in the refrigerator should be safe to eat for four to five weeks after they were packed, and for a couple of weeks after the "sell by" date.

- **Grade:** Refers to the quality of the egg. Most consumers won't notice much of a difference among the grades. You'll most likely see Grade A or AA, which means the shells are unstained, the yolks are free from defects and the eggs have a "reasonably" clear and thick white. Grade B usually go to institutional egg users, such as food-service kitchens and commercial bakeries.

- **Size:** Refers to the weight of whole eggs per dozen. (*EatingWell* almost always calls for large eggs in recipes.)

- **Free-Range:** The USDA defines free-range eggs as eggs that come from hens housed in a building, room or area that allows for unlimited access to food,

water and the outdoors during their laying cycle. The outdoor area may be fenced or covered with netting-like material. As with cage-free, there are no minimum space requirements or "furnishings," nor any standards for how hens can exit the building.

- **Organic:** Hens are uncaged, free to roam in their houses and have access to the outdoors. They eat an organic diet. But there are no animal welfare standards beyond that. And 80 percent of organic eggs are currently produced in industrial-style farms where hens have little access to the outside (sometimes only a small covered "porch"), says a Cornucopia Institute report. The USDA has a proposed rule pending with more guidance on living conditions and animal treatment.

- **No Hormones:** Farmers are not allowed to give hormones to hens, so this label can only be used if it is followed by a statement like "Federal regulations prohibit the use of hormones," which can be in tiny print or indicated by an asterisk somewhere else on the package.

- **No Antibiotics:** Producers must provide the USDA with documentation proving the hens are raised without antibiotics. Most well-managed facilities don't use antibiotics, say poultry experts, because the drugs would get into the eggs, which is prohibited. It's common, however, to vaccinate hens against contagious diseases.

- **United Egg Producers Certified:** UEP is the egg companies' trade group and stipulates how birds are handled, transported, euthanized, etc. It certifies over 80 percent of caged birds, so this seal pretty much means the chickens are treated as they have always been treated. For example, hens can be raised in as little as 67 square inches of space each (that's a little larger than an 8-inch square).

- **American Humane Certified:** The American Humane Association certifies egg producers with its own standards for caged, cage-free and enriched colony housing (a type of cage that contains perches, scratch pads and nest boxes). They're better than UEP standards, but not as rigorous as those of other animal welfare groups.

- **Certified Humane:** Humane Farm Animal Care requires no cages (ever). Hens must be able to dust-bathe, perch and have secluded nest boxes, among other requirements. Each hen has at minimum 1 square foot of space.

- **Animal Welfare Approved:** These are the most rigorous standards. All birds are cage-free and get at least 4 square feet each and have continuous outdoor access. The maximum flock size is 500 birds and only family farms can participate (the family owns the birds, works the farm and makes all or part of their livelihood from the hens).

- **Omega-3 Enriched:** Laid by hens that are fed a special diet with added omega-3 fatty acids from flaxseed. The eggs provide a range of omega-3s, from 100 mg to over 600 mg per egg. (For comparison, 3 ounces of salmon has about 1,200 mg omega-3s.)

- **Pasteurized:** These eggs are heated in their shells to a temperature just high enough to destroy pathogens like *Salmonella*. If you want to consume them raw, pasteurized eggs are a smart choice.

- **Pasture-Raised:** There are no specific guidelines or third-party audits for "pasture-raised," nor is it USDA-regulated.

- **Natural:** Nothing is added to eggs, so all eggs are "natural," says the USDA.

- **Vegetarian-Fed:** Some third parties have stipulations around vegetarian feed, but the term isn't USDA-regulated. Plus, chickens are omnivores, so eating bugs, worms or even small animals is natural (and key for certain nutrients).

INDEX

SPECIAL-INTEREST INDEXES

GLUTEN-FREE
Does not include wheat, barley, rye, or any ingredient that contains or is derived from one of these ingredients (e.g., triticale, spelt, kamut, farina, wheat bran, durum flour, enriched flour and semolina). Recipes including oats or ingredients derived from oats (e.g., oat bran) are also excluded, as contamination during growing or processing of oats is common. Check the labels of processed foods to make sure they don't contain hidden sources of gluten.

VEGETARIAN & VEGAN

Meatless (e.g., no meat, poultry, or seafood) includes meatless options and contains no ingredients derived from these meat-based products (e.g., gelatin, animal-based broths, fish or oyster sauce). These recipes may still include eggs, egg products, butter and milk, or other dairy-containing products.

*Recipes marked with an asterisk are also vegan, based on their omission of all animal-based products (e.g., meat, poultry, fish, milk, and eggs) and ingredients from animal sources (i.e., butter, lard, gelatin, fish or oyster sauce, animal-based broths, etc.). Check the label of ingredients to make sure they do not contain any hidden sources of animal products.

CONTRIBUTORS

Our thanks to these fine food writers and recipe developers whose work was previously published in *EatingWell* magazine.

Nancy Baggett | Chilly Dilly Cucumber Soup, 199

Jane Black | Mascarpone-Stuffed Figs, 231

April Bloomfield | Roasted Carrots with Garlic Confit & Thyme, 166

David Bonom | Tofu & Vegetable Stew, 40; Bean & Barley Soup, 201

Carolyn Casner | Seared Salmon with Green Peppercorn Sauce, 29; Carne Asada Tacos, 74; Quick "Corned" Beef & Cabbage, 112; Braised Cauliflower & Squash Penne Pasta, 121; Apple & Grilled Chicken Salad with Cheddar Toasts, 154; Beet & Shrimp Winter Salad, 206; Mango-Date Energy Bites, 218

Stacy Fraser | Roasted Tofu & Peanut Noodle Salad, 44; Oven-Fried Beef Taquitos, 103; Cashew & 3-Seed Chocolate Bark, 227; Instant Mango Frozen Yogurt, 242

Darra Goldstein | Pineapple & Avocado Salad, 170

Kathy Gunst | Fish with Coconut-Shallot Sauce, 78; Broiled Ginger-Lime Chicken, 81; Baked Eggs, Tomatoes & Chiles (Shakshuka), 86

Sara Haas, R.D.N., L.D.N. | Roast Pork, Asparagus & Cherry Tomato Bowl, 67; Mediterranean Tuna-Spinach Salad, 209

Joyce Hendley | Moroccan Lentil Soup, 202; Homemade Trail Mix, 217

Emily Horton | Spiced Apple Bread Pudding, 236

Lia Huber | Roasted Chicken & Vegetable Quinoa Salad, 59; Beef & Bulgur Burgers with Blue Cheese, 60; Two-Pepper Shrimp with Creamy Pecorino Oats, 63

Breana Lai | Za'atar-Roasted Chicken Tenders & Vegetables with Couscous, 64; Kale & White Bean Potpie with Chive Biscuits, 97; Sweet Potato Macaroni & Cheese, 104; Crispy Chicken Schnitzel with Herb-Brown Butter, 108; Spanakopita Loaded Potatoes, 111; Paprika Chicken Thighs with Brussels Sprouts, 124

Carolyn Malcoun | Cherry, Wild Rice & Quinoa Salad, 61; Skillet Swiss Steak, 120; Chimichurri Grilled Steak Salad, 142; Grilled Chicken with Blueberry-Lime Salsa, 153; Pork Fajitas with Smoky Cherry Salsa, 159; Mini Blueberry-Lemon Cheesecakes, 239; Cherry Sorbet, 241

Hilary Meyer | 8-Layer Taco Salad, 100; Creamy Turnip Soup, 118; Spicy Tunisian Grilled Chicken, 141

Jason Mraz | Jason Mraz's Avocado Green Smoothie, 190; "Chocomole" Pudding, 228

Seamus Mullen | Sugar Snap Pea Salad, 169

Laraine Perri | Roasted Halibut with Tangerine & Olive Tapenade, 85

Jim Romanoff | Black-Eyed Pea Dip, 210

Julee Rosso | Pistachio Breakfast Sausage Patties, 186

Becky Selengut | Grilled Salmon with Watercress Salad & Buttermilk Dressing, 157

Marie Simmons | Farrotto with Artichokes, 56; Savory Prosciutto Muffins, 182; Double Corn-Blueberry Cobbler, 235; Apricot Grunt, 240

Michael Solomonov | Asparagus Tabbouleh, 165

Jan Ellen Spiegel | Potato, Asparagus & Mushroom Hash, 185

Robb Walsh | Mom's Chili, 135

Katie Workman | Shrimp & Vegetable Red Rice Salad, 68

By the Editors of *EatingWell*

For more than 20 years, *EatingWell* magazine has been at the forefront of what Americans now embrace: the rewards of eating better. *EatingWell* delivers delicious recipes, balanced nutritional advice, thought-provoking stories and new ways to make healthy choices exciting. The very best recipes, photos and science-backed tips from our experts go into each *EatingWell* cookbook. For more great *EatingWell* food, visit us at EatingWell.com.

FACEBOOK:
facebook.com/EatingWell

INSTAGRAM & TWITTER:
@EatingWell

PINTEREST:
pinterest.com/eatingwell

COVER DESIGN: Jan Derevjanik
COVER PHOTOGRAPHS: Helen Norman (front); Jim Westphalen (back)

EAT BETTER EVERY DAY

EatingWell Quick & Clean is packed with clear, sensible information and delicious recipes that really work. Created by the editors of *EatingWell* magazine, this book draws on the knowledge of a team of registered dietitians, an academic advisory panel and Test Kitchen experts. That means you can trust that the advice on everything from how to improve your diet to what to buy at the market is science-backed and no-nonsense.

Inside are more than 100 easy and achievable recipes that feature short ingredient lists and focus on whole foods that are easy to find. Almost all take fewer than 45 minutes start to finish, and there's even a chapter devoted to 20-minute dinners. Beyond dinner, you'll find packable recipes for breakfast, lunch and snacks that work with any schedule. Taste recipes like Asparagus Tabbouleh, Seared Chicken with Lemon-Herb Cream Sauce and Double Corn–Blueberry Cobbler, and you'll see just how delicious clean eating can be.

$22.00 / HIGHER IN CANADA
ISBN 978-0-544-92550-2

Houghton Mifflin Harcourt | www.hmhco.com
© Houghton Mifflin Harcourt Publishing Company

52200

9 780544 925502

1656879